BROKEN RUNGS

Yet I Climbed

Revised Edition

Mary G. Patton, Ph.D.

BOOKS ACADEMY

LEARNING LIFE FROM EVERY PAGE

Books Academy LLC
112 SW H K Dodgen Loop
Temple, Texas 76504
Hotline: (254) 800-1189
Ordering Information:
Quantity sales. Special discounts are available on quantity purchases by corporations, associations, and others. For details, contact the publisher at the address above.

Printed in the United States of America.

ISBN-13:   Paperback   978-1-964929-77-4
                eBook   978-1-964929-78-1

Library of Congress Control Number: 2024924961

And we know that all things work together for good to those who love God, to those who are the called according to His purpose.

—Romans 8:28 (NKJV)

CONTENTS

ACKNOWLEDGEMENTS

To my husband, Elder Norris Patton, my girls, Norrissia Hope Hightower and Ulrica Rachelle Dunmeyer, grandsons, Xavier N. Jones, Norris T. J. Patton, Amari E. J. Dunmeyer, Alijah K. Z. Dunmeyer, and our great-grandson, Xyzon L. Patton—you are the joys of my heart, and my constant inspiration for embracing life to its fullest. Thank you for motivating me to write this book. Thanks to my girls (Hope and Rae) for assisting with proofreading my many revisions; and to Hope and my son-in-law, Jonathan Dunmeyer, for assisting with my photo selections and preparations.

A huge appreciation goes to my little sister, Debra Patterson-Brown. My list of photos would have been incomplete without your help in searching through Momma's old photo albums.

To my cousin, Pearlie Childs, thank you for the many hours spent driving my dear aunts to visit. Because of your unselfishness and love of family, I have many special memories that helped to inspire this book.

To my grandpa, Louis W. Patterson, Jr., daddy, Pinkney E. Patterson, momma, Martha L. Myles-Patterson, granddaughter, Thalira M. Chupp, and aunts Annie Ruth Myles-Johnson and Ethel Mae Myles-Childs—I will carry your memories in my heart forever and thank each of you sincerely for the legacies of love and spiritual insight that you left me. They have served as personal gateways to learning some of my most valuable life lessons.

Thanks to Dr. Bartholomew Orr, Dr. Wyvonia Woods Harris, and Carmen Kyle, for their kindness and support by endorsing the back cover of my book.

To my author support person, Lucy Parker, and her team, thank you for being there with a smile throughout my many revisions. Your support and kindness have been truly appreciated. I feel like you personally held my hand as we worked together to ensure a quality book.

Most of all, I thank God for His loving mercy that is shown to me daily.

PREFACE

Everyone has their story. Mine is a factual account of many Broken Rungs. My story chronicles the grace that God extended to me and gives numerous examples of how that grace has provided a source of hope, help, and healing as I struggled to navigate through some of the most difficult and painful stages of life from childhood well into adulthood. I've learned that we never outgrow our need for His grace. My hope is that as you read through the pages of this book, your spiritual insight will be sharpened, permitting you to perceive His grace as it guides my life and connect with me as we travel through some memories together. My further hope is that as we make our journey side-by-side, you will experience a consciousness of the grace that orchestrated my life and share the experience that moved me through and around each of those devastating obstacles by which I was confronted.

I have faith that each of those obstacles was designed to draw me closer to my destiny. My further desire is that, as you read my story, you will also recognize the grace of God that is being presently extended to assist you as you confront those difficult periods of your life. I pray that you will surrender to His power, as I learned to do, and trust in that power as it composes the story of your life events that have been designed to usher you into your destiny as well.

The Bible speaks to a promise recorded in Matthew 11:28 (NKJV) that if those of us who are weary and burdened would come to Him, our Lord, He would give us rest. It is my personal experience that the promised rest is from anxiety, depression, fear, grief, and whatever else that may cause my heart to experience discontent. In my opinion, rest in this context is synonymous with peace. For me, emotions such as anxiety, depression, fear, and grief have been peace robbers. They tended to invade my mind when I least expected and took away that sweet rest/peace that was promised to me in the Scriptures.

I likened my life story to a ladder that was not in good condition, making it impossible and, to say the least, difficult to climb. I chose this similarity because from the very beginning there seemed to have always been a struggle to get from one level to the next. I compared my life to a ladder that had numerous broken rungs, making it appear to be discarded and useless to those who viewed it. The crucial word in that sentence is appear. My life experiences have taught me very valuable lessons, one being that we must not quit because a task looks impossible, but rather keep working diligently, with an open ear to the leading of the Holy Spirit, because many things are not as they initially appear to be.

HIS PLAN

**"For I know the plans I have for you," declares
the Lord, "plans to prosper you and not to harm
you, plans to give you hope and a future..."
—Jeremiah 28:11 NIV**

I was supposed to have been just another unfortunate statistic, but God had a plan for me. In various discussions, I have heard individuals as they advance in their chosen career fields make statements to the effect that they were climbing the ladder of success. Climbing that proverbial ladder to success in life can be an exciting adventure if the climber is fortunate enough to have been presented with a ladder that is in good condition. For a successful climb, an individual would expect to use a ladder that is equipped with ample rungs in place to acquire proper footing with which to move safely from one level to the next. The climb can be an extremely challenging task to perform if the ladder that is expected to be the major tool for navigating our journey through life has many severely damaged rungs.

Attempting to climb when there are numerous broken rungs can be a tremendously tedious and dangerous struggle. There is the potential of falling and sustaining an injury that could delay one's climb or end it all together. In some instances, the rung may appear to be intact until the weight of the climber is applied. Breaks are not always visible to an enthusiastic climber who has his or her eyes fixed on the prize at the top. The same is true with our lives. We often assume that we are safe and have things under control until the weights of life are applied. Those weights come in the form of disappointments, stress, anxiety, grief, and other painful realities that result from living life from day to day. It is usually not until a certain amount of pressure has been applied that we become cognizant something is broken. It is at that moment of awareness when our footing begins to slip, and the foundation that we thought was sufficiently supporting us shatters. This is the actual moment that fear, insecurity, and anxiety produced from attempting to climb a broken ladder becomes painfully apparent. The struggle to make sense out of the shattered pieces of our dreams can take many paths, each of which has the potential to intensify those emotionally debilitating feelings that we regularly attempt to suppress in a futile effort to appear unscathed to those who may have been onlookers when our life-altering fall occurred.

That is precisely how my story began. My ladder of success did not appear conducive for climbing at all and was presented to me extremely early in life. It contained various rungs that were cracked, missing, and broken. That damaged ladder to success created countless obstacles that were intended to prevent a successful climb. According to recent statistics, I was doomed for failure even before I was born.

My odds for achieving anything resembling what is now considered to be a successful life had been stacked against me in several ways, one of which was the fact that I was born to teen parents. My mother was a mere child herself. She was going to be fifteen years old in three months when she gave birth to me on a cold night in January as she lay frightened, screaming in pain on a pallet of quilts that my grandmother had made to serve as her birthing area. Many years later, after I had become an adult, she laughed as we talked about her experience. She said she was eating a plate of rutabagas that she had been craving and, when the labor pains hit, her plate of rutabaga went one way, and she went the other. Even though she laughingly told me that story, I'm sure it was no laughing matter when the actual event occurred. She told me her pallet had been placed on the floor in front of their wood-burning fireplace in the little country shack that was home for them. I am guessing it might have been placed near the fireplace for warmth or perhaps to aid the kerosene lamp in providing light for the midwife to see well enough to perform her duties of ushering me into the world. Momma wasn't sure why she was positioned near the fireplace. I'm simply speculating as to why.

My mother did not have the luxury of a carpeted floor as many of us enjoy today. She had a simple wood floor covered with a linoleum rug. It must have been very hard. I can also imagine that, in addition, it must have been rather cold. Those little shanties that poor farmers occupied were not well-made. They had very little or no insulation at all. In their effort to prevent some of the cold air from coming into the house and to contain as much heat as possible, they often had to stuff rags underneath the door and around the windows.

My young mother struggled with excruciating pain in a primitive and unsterile environment to give birth with the assistance of a midwife who probably had no formal training. She did not have the availability of pain medication to minimize her suffering as is accessible to mothers today, nor had she been educated in terms of how to breathe with the contractions to ease her pain. The Lamaze method of childbirth had not yet been heard of. She had to endure the entire excruciatingly painful process of labor and delivery without any assistance. A kerosene lamp and embers in the fireplace provided the only light available to the midwife who assisted me in making my entrance to the world that cold winter night in January.

I often wondered if my birth may have been bittersweet for my mother because her brother had been recently murdered, and his funeral arrangements conflicted with the time of my birth. Momma did not get a chance to attend the funeral. During that time, new mothers remained homebound for at least a month before taking their infants out in public.

The enjoyment of having her baby girl may undoubtedly have, on occasion, been mingled with tears of sadness and grief. I pondered the idea that perhaps my birthdate would be a yearly reminder of the murder and of the fact that she was not able to attend that funeral and say her last goodbye. I'm speculating again about her feelings in terms of missing the funeral because she never discussed them with anyone. Whatever feelings she had in terms of that whole incident went with her to the grave. Momma did not speak about her emotional pain, but she often wore it on her face as some wear makeup. Her pain was visible to those who knew her well. It was as if she had resigned herself to believing that living in pain was her lot in life. The only emotion that I can remember her talking about was anger. She not only spoke of it but expressed it from time to time. I've come to understand anger as a replacement emotion, one that is often used as a substitute for pain because to acknowledge pain reveals vulnerability. Momma was a very proud and strong woman. She never wanted to reveal even the slightest amount of weakness.

I think Momma may have had unresolved issues that developed from childhood feelings resulting from the loss of her mother. The fact that she was a young child, home alone with her mother when she died surely must have impacted her in some way. Momma shared with me that a few years after her mother's death, she had been forced to get married at age thirteen because she was falsely accused of being pregnant. Momma had kept those thoughts buried inside her mind for years, never speaking about them until just a couple of years before she died. My young mother had not had much modeling in terms of parenting when I was born, which probably placed me in even more of a high-risk category for failure.

My father was eighteen years old when I entered the family. He had been drafted into the military to serve in World War II and had already left for training when I made my arrival into the world. He was not there to support nor share the joy with his young wife upon the arrival of their first child. He was not around for those 3:00 a.m. feedings, to see me take my first step, or to see my first tooth push its way through. He missed out on that critical bonding period that is believed to be extremely important for a child's healthy development.

My father's absence undoubtably created a void in my life. However, that void was lovingly filled by my grandpa. My mother lived in the house with my grandparents and was parented along with my aunts and uncles who were teenagers at the time. I was told that Daddy came home from the army when I was approximately two years old, and I asked, "Who is that?"

After his discharge from the military, my parents moved into their own little place. Grandpa had been the strong, loving, and supportive male figure that I needed during those early months of development and beyond. He and I shared a very special bond, one that my father and I were never quite able to achieve.

Not only did I have a teen mother who knew nothing about parenting, and a teen father who knew even less and with whom I was unable to bond, I was born to a teen mother who had received no pre-natal care. At the time when I entered the world, poor people could not afford to acquire proper medical care, and there were no social programs available for sharecroppers. Therefore, pre-natal care was unheard of.

My family relied on home remedies for everything. Whenever someone was sick or hurt, my grandmother would create a special treatment, usually from some herb found growing in the wild. The skill of using home remedies was passed down to my mother, and she practiced the art quite successfully for many years. Even after proper medical care became available to her, she preferred to use some of her home remedies.

Research indicates that children born under the conditions that I was are usually low-birth-weight and are prone to have physical or cognitive problems. That was not the case with me. Instead, I was a healthy baby and thrived in all areas of development. The fact that I grew up in poverty was yet another broken rung on my ladder to success, and one of the obstacles that the grace of God was going to bring me through.

I am so grateful that *when God appoints, and anoints us for His service, adverse circumstances do not have power to abort His plan!* When God is at work in our lives, He tends to use tools to prepare us for His intended purposes that others often deem as trash, making it crystal clear that it is His mighty hand that is orchestrating the plan. He makes it known to all who have been gifted with spiritual insight that it does not matter how we begin our climb. What makes the climb impactful is when He directs the process. We must be careful and not allow ourselves to be deceived by our circumstances. It's imperative that we strive to remember the fact that our lives have purpose and matters greatly to God. He will not allow those whom He has appointed for His service to be defined by their environment, and for that I am enormously grateful!

MY PURPOSE

"Before I formed you in the womb, I knew you; Before you
were Born I sanctified you…"
—Jeremiah1:5 (NKJV)

As that Scripture indicates, God knew and sanctified
Jeremiah before he was conceived in his mother's womb, and it
further indicates to me that our lives have meaning even before
conception. What an awesome revelation it is to realize that He also
knew and sanctified me for His purpose before placing me in the
womb of a poverty-stricken, emotionally-scarred teenage girl. She
was destined to be my mother. God had a specific purpose for me
just as He does for every little girl or boy born into the world. The
conditions surrounding a baby's birth does not alter how God plans
to use his/her life. Just like Jeremiah, we all were born for a specific
purpose.

When I fully comprehended the realization of being
destined for His use, even before conception, that blew my mind.
My life began to make some sense. Understanding that spiritual
concept in Jeremiah clarified for me why I was presented at birth
with a ladder consisting of so many broken rungs. I now realized
that the work I was destined to perform required specialized skills.
Those skills required strategic training for effective use. My birth
and consequential life experiences provided me with the necessary
conditioning and strength training for the assignment that I
believed was my divine destiny. Every obstacle that I faced
revealed a blueprint for my calling in life. It is exciting now that I
am finally able to connect the dots.

I believe that the Holy Spirit was educating me for a divinely appointed career. For every career, there is a period of preparation. More sensitive work responsibilities often require more intense training. To successfully accomplish the work that I believe God appointed me to do, it was imperative for me to become highly skilled in areas such as patience, endurance, forgiveness, love, empathy, and sensitivity. I didn't know it then, but my life's work would be to provide tools necessary for restoring hope and healing to those suffering from emotional wounds resulting from broken hearts, and the aforementioned character traits are some of the qualities that always require restoring in the hearts and minds of those suffering from emotional distress resulting from broken hearts.

The lessons that I learned from my past experiences were specifically designed to provide me with real-time knowledge of what it felt like to be broken. If I were to be effective in facilitating healing the hurt of other individuals, then I needed to experience hurt along with the liberating process of being healed from that hurt myself. When we have first-hand knowledge of circumstances, we are better equipped to speak about them with increased authority and conviction. I think that my experiences prepared me to speak as an expert.

When we experience painful situations and have healed successfully, I believe that the process of going through those experiences makes it easier to empathize with others who are dealing with a similar event. I've come to further believe that every individual experience holds a lesson to be learned for living a more productive and victorious life, and that our lessons learned are not usually intended just for our personal purposes but are to be shared with others for the benefit of assisting them in living their best lives as well.

I don't believe that a God who is omniscient will ever do anything frivolously but rather does all things with intention. I am confident that He used my teen parents to put a plan into action that would demonstrate His great power to heal and deliver so that I, and anyone else who may have doubted the possibility of overcoming unsurmountable obstacles, may become acquainted with His power and understand that, with Him as our source, nothing is ever impossible. We may often bend from the burdens of life, but He will never permit us to break.

My mother shared stories with me about when I was a baby, and how much joy I brought to the family as the first grandchild. She described me as having chubby cheeks and very little hair. She said that even though I had only a few strands on the top of my head, she always managed to tie a ribbon on them every time she took me out. I remember seeing my photo as a baby many years ago. I was wearing a bonnet which prevented me from seeing the strands of hair she referred to. Regrettably, that photo was misplaced, and we never found it again.

My mother said that I was a beautiful, happy baby. I could see a twinkle of joy in her eyes every time she shared those stories. She shared stories about walking trips to town with another young mother who had a baby about my age. Momma said as they approached town, they always switched babies at the other woman's suggestion. She said the other young mother received a lot of attention for the baby she was carrying whereas Momma didn't get any attention for the baby she was carrying. She told me that story several times and laughed heartily with each account admitting that she didn't figure out what was going on until much later. She also shared stories of how my grandpa bounced me on his knee and sang songs that he would make up especially for me. She told me that he gave me a nickname of Pie Jaws because of my chubby cheeks. I never doubted my grandpa's fondness for me and can honestly say that each of my interactions with him were positive ones from the time I was able to remember him until he transitioned this life.

She told me a story involving my father that happened when I was a toddler. She wasn't sure how old I was at the time, but she remembered that they were planting sweet potato plants. She said that, as they were planting, I was coming behind them, pulling up the plants. Apparently, I thought I was helping since I was very young and obviously had no perception of what I was doing. She said Daddy wanted to spank me for pulling up the plants, but my grandmother would not allow him to do so. She apparently knew that there was a better way to teach me that what I was doing was not helping them. Daddy—in true Daddy fashion—was determined to have his way. Momma said that he picked me up and ran with me spanking my legs as he ran to get away from my grandmother who was running after him in the effort to stop him from hitting me. I'm sure that an emphatic no was all he needed to teach me that I was not being helpful. He certainly could have benefited from some parenting lessons because his inappropriate parenting choices continued for many years after that incident.

Listening to the stories that Momma shared provided me an opportunity to reflect on how thoroughly I was convinced that I had been favored by God and further solidified my faith that I had been selected for a specific assignment in life just as Jeremiah had been. The happy stories as well as those not-so-happy ones revealed to me the power and protection of a very deliberate God.

PART I

**In everything give thanks; for this is the will of God in
Christ Jesus for you.
—1 Thessalonians 5:18 (NKJV)**

One of my earliest memories was when I was about four
years old and living on a plantation. It was several miles
from town and approximately a mile-and-a-half from the
major highway in a remote area, near a small body of water. I can
remember about four poorly-constructed houses, ours included, that
were on that plot of land. They were all on the same side of the road,
and there was a significant amount of space between each one used
as a cotton field. I remember smaller plots of land that did not have
cotton and were set aside for each family to grow food. Those areas
were called either a truck patch or garden depending upon the size
of the plot of land. Smaller plots were usually gardens whereas the
larger plots were the truck patches. The scene of the potato plants
story had taken place in the family truck patch.

I remember a wooded area with a lot of trees in the distance
in front of our house and along the banks of the water area. Daddy
would go to those woods every year around Christmas time and chop
down a little evergreen for our Christmas tree. Momma and I would
make paper chains for decoration. She used cotton balls for snow
on the tree and around the base of the tree for a skirt.

She always cut a cardboard star and covered it with aluminum foil to adorn the top of our little tree. That tradition has remained with me. I adorn the top of my Christmas tree with a star to this day. Christmas was always a favorite time of the year for Momma and me.

I remember Daddy going hunting in that wooded area as well. I don't know if he enjoyed the sport of hunting or if he did it because we needed the food. Mostly he would come home with rabbits after his hunting expeditions, but on occasions he brought home a squirrel, raccoon, or an opossum. Whatever he had in his hunting bag Momma made a meal out of it.

In our yard was a cistern that collected rainwater. The water was used for drinking, bathing, and doing laundry. A bucket attached to a rope was used to draw water from the cistern. It was a miracle that we didn't contract a deadly disease from drinking that unsanitary water. I remember it often contained mosquito larva that could be seen swimming around in the bucket, and I can only imagine what else was in that cistern! I shudder at the thought of what may have been down there.

Our house was close to a graveled road that extended from the main highway throughout the rural area. We had a mailbox in front of our house, surprisingly I can even remember the route number. It's amazing the things that we remember from our childhood. I guess I remember the mailbox because it was what seemingly kept us connected with the rest of the family that lived in other places. Occasionally the mailman would bring a letter from a family member that we had not seen in a long time. That was always exciting for my parents.

We lived in a little shanty that consisted of one room, a kitchen, and a front porch. The multi-purpose room served as our sitting room and bedroom. My parent's bed was on one side and my bed was on the other side of the room. An antiquated cast iron wood-burning heater in the middle of the room warmed us during the cold winter months. An old wardrobe was positioned on the wall next to the door that led to the porch. We had three straight-backed wooden chairs for sitting and one rocking chair. I remember a piece of wire extending across one corner of the room and that was used to hang our clothes on. It was always covered by a sheet. I assume that was to protect the items from collecting dust.

My father used rubber from a discarded automobile tire innertube to make the chair bottoms. With incredible skill, he made perfect lattice from the rubber, and the chairs were comfortable to sit on. We only had three of those straight-backed chairs because we were a family of three. If anyone came by to visit, they would sit on the chairs, and I would sit on the bed or go outside to play while the grown-ups talked. At that time children were not allowed to interject into adult conversation unless they were asked a question.

On the other side of the room was a door which led to the little kitchen that contained a wood burning stove and several tin cans that held flour, sugar, meal, rice, cane syrup, and lard. The very large tin cans sat on the floor and the smaller ones were neatly arranged on a shelf that was attached to the wall with nails. I remember a white ice box in the kitchen that looked like an old refrigerator. It had a small compartment at the top, and the larger one was at the bottom. The ice box usually had no ice but was available when there was money to purchase ice from the ice-man when he came by in his ice truck or when daddy brought some home from the ice house in town. The ice box helped to keep food from spoiling from the heat and for cooling pitchers of iced tea on occasions. The little shanty had a tin roof which contributed to the sweltering heat during summer months that was intensified in the kitchen and into the other room when my mother made meals.

Our table always had a colorful oil-cloth table cover on it. We didn't have much, but what we did have was always neat and clean. My mother had a flair for decorating and used what she could find to make the place as attractive as possible. Those three straight-backed chairs did double duty. They served in the kitchen and in the "house" as the multi-purpose room was often referred to.

Some of my fondest memories of that time were with my grandpa. We spent many enjoyable times together. Whenever he was not working or at church, we could be found fishing in the little stream that was called the "ditch." Grandpa loved to fish, and I just loved being with him. Fishing was never my passion. I enjoyed being with my grandpa, listening to the stories that he would always tell. He was an avid reader, with a fantastic memory. It was as if he had memorized every one of Grimm's fairy tales. He would recite one after another for me after we shared our special "fishing-time" together. The family often gathered together with Grandpa some evenings for Storytime. When we fished together, Grandpa would bait my hook because I was afraid of worms. He would also take off my hook anything that I happened to catch. Sometimes it would be a fish, and other times it would be a crawfish. It didn't matter to me what was on the hook, I was not about to touch it. Grandpa seemed to know that and would always gently take my pole and remove my catch while continuing to talk about something that made me laugh. My Grandpa was the best. He was always very gentle, patient, and kind. Unlike daddy, Grandpa never once raised his voice at me or became impatient. He had a way of making me feel as though I was the most important little girl in the whole world.

I remember the cold winters living in our little shanty. Daddy would cut wood to make the fire in the cast-iron heater. I can recall helping him saw logs into blocks of wood that he would split into thinner pieces with his ax to use in the heater. I remember getting scolded for what he called *riding the saw*. I thought that the harder I pressed down, the faster we would cut through the log. Apparently, the harder I pressed down, the more difficult it was for him to pull his end of the saw through the log, and he didn't like that. Whenever I pressed down too hard, Daddy would let me know in no uncertain terms that I needed to stop *riding the saw.*

When it snowed, which was not very often, my parents would take some snow, mix it with sugar, vanilla, and a bit of milk for a tasty treat that we called snow cream. Daddy would make a trap to catch birds that came up on the front porch to eat corn kernels or breadcrumbs that he enticed them with. My parents took the feathers off and prepared them for cooking. It wasn't much meat but, evidently, they thought that the birds were worth the effort.

I remember the hot summers. My uncle, who was my playmate, and best friend at the time, would come to play in the front yard under the chinaberry tree. I remember getting hit with retracting limbs often in my effort to climb that big old tree. I guess I never quite learned the art of quitting and never gave up until I climbed just as far up as my uncle did. I never have learned the art of quitting, and that has worked in my favor. Once I start a project, I usually finish if it is at all possible.

My uncle and I played horseback-riding using broomsticks as our horses. That was as close to horseback riding as I ever came, since I was, and to this day am, afraid of horses. I remember our trips to the woods where fruit seemingly grew wild. If it is true that seeds produce of their own kind, then someone at some point must have planted those fruit seeds. That was another one of my childhood mysteries that was never solved. We picked blackberries, persimmons, and plums that grew in the wooded area near our home.

Even though I was very young at the time, my life was jam-packed with complications.

PART II

To everything there is a season, a time for every purpose under the heaven.
—Ecclesiastes 3:1 (NKJV)

I remember starting school when I was five years old. The regular age to begin school at that time was six years. Kindergarten did not exist, but we had two years of what was called primer. Students were assigned a pre-primer during the first year of school, and a big-primer the second year. After completing both primers, students were assigned to first grade. Most of the students had a fair start on reading at that point.

My uncle and I were very close and did everything together. He was a year older. When he turned six and was ready for school, I went along with my grandmother to register him. When he was issued a book, I don't remember the incident, but my grandmother said that I wanted one too and cried bitterly until the teacher told her that I could come to school along with my uncle. She issued me the pre-primer mostly to appease me and just to see how I would handle it. I may not have been of age to begin school, but I was most definitely ready. I completed the pre-primer much faster than the teacher anticipated, and she gave me the big-primer which I also competed much faster than she expected. What was usually a two-year study, I had completed in one.

That placed me ahead of my peers and my uncle academically. I believe that God was showing me His favor early in life. The child born to a teen mother with no pre-natal care was not intellectually challenged, as modern statistics may indicate, but was performing ahead of her peers. I defied the odds and successfully climbed another broken rung on my ladder to success.

I continued to defy the odds that appeared to have been stacked against me, by excelling in school. I consistently remained at the top of my class, and Momma was bursting with pride.

I attended a little one-room church school until fourth grade. There were no school buses at the time. Therefore, my uncles, aunt, and I walked to school each day. The walk was several miles. The church school was located on the main highway at the top of a huge hill that appeared to be a mountain to me, as a little girl. Rather than walk on the side of the busy highway, we often used a trail that was several feet away from the highway and ran across the top of that huge hill. The walk was always fun. We ran and played often sliding down the side of the hill toward the highway. It was only the grace of God that none of us accidentally slid onto the highway and got struck by a car.

School was a lot of fun. We had May Day celebrations and a little competitive marching band that I was a part of. The teacher took us on nature walks and picnics. I participated in school plays and enjoyed everything about school, even though I was always nervous when I had to perform or speak in front of a group. Nonetheless, I managed to do it and did it well. I always wanted to make my parents and grandparents proud of me. I developed the need to please from a very early age. That need to please later became one of my struggles to overcome as I grew older. My need to please turned out to be a broken rung.

I got along well with the students at school except one. There was one girl who would challenge me to a fight almost every day. Now that I think of it, she would have been considered the school bully, but the term bully was not popular during those times. I was not afraid of her, perhaps that was why she challenged me frequently. Bullies like to arouse fear in their victims. My father had taught me to take care of myself. He drilled it into my mind that I was not to start a fight, but I was not to run away from one either. He taught me that if anyone ever hit me, I should always hit them back. My uncle was my backup. If I got into trouble that I could not handle on my own, he would immediately come to my rescue. As I reflect on my father's advice, I realize now that it was neither sound nor Godly. We went to Sunday school every Sunday, but he never taught me what it meant to turn the other cheek or the value in being a peacemaker. Walking away from a fight required wisdom and maturity. Those were qualities that my young father had not developed at that point in his life.

I had one best friend at school. We played together every day, and occasionally we visited each other's home on Sundays after church. I remember my friend being even-tempered, gentle, and forgiving. My temperament appeared to be the opposite of hers, yet we got along well most of the time. I was kindhearted and sometimes had a gentle spirit. I had a temper and struggled to control it even from a young age. I often would become enraged whenever I felt wronged and later would feel extremely hurt and ashamed of my angry outbursts and negative behavior. My behavior was indicative of an abused child, but no one knew at that time anything about child abuse or its residuals.

I remember one time when I lost my temper and behaved very badly toward my friend. My mother had bought me a new winter coat. It was identical to my friend's coat except hers was not new. She had rips in the lining of her coat and that was how we were able to know our coats apart. Since we were friends, we always hung our coats beside each other on the coat rack.

9

One day, as we were leaving school, she took my coat from the rack and went home. When I discovered that she had my new coat instead of her own and that I had to wear hers home, I became enraged. I accused her of taking my coat on purpose because I did not understand how she could not have known the difference. The lining in her coat was torn. She must've noticed that there were no rips in the lining of the coat when she put it on. I was thinking, how could she not have noticed that she had my coat? I felt like she had taken something away from me that I valued very much, and in my angry rage, I began to rip her coat lining even more. My uncle joined in, and we tore the lining almost completely out of her coat.

By the time I arrived home, I was no longer angry and already feeling awful about what my uncle and I had done. My anxiety was mounting in terms of what my father would do to me because of my behavior, in addition to how I was going to face my friend and explain to her what we had done to her coat. She was my friend, and I didn't want to lose our friendship. I didn't understand my temper flare-ups then. However, looking back with the insight of a counseling psychologist, I now realize that many of my early childhood experiences had been forms of abuse. My anger issues, which tended to explode out of control any time I found myself in a position of helplessness, situations that were beyond my control, were residuals of abuse that I had experienced and continued to endure from time to time.

Daddy had taught me to protect myself but ripping my friend's coat was not protecting myself. That was destruction of someone's property for which I had no excuse and was severely punished. Daddy gave me a harsh tongue lashing, accompanied by a whipping. I had to face my friend the next day and apologize for my behavior. Daddy had a talk with her parents.

The adults worked it out between themselves, and my friend and I worked things out between ourselves. Thankfully she forgave me, and our friendship has remained stable. I was very grateful that she forgave me. I learned a valuable lesson from that experience and have not destroyed anyone's property since that time, regardless of the intensity of my anger episodes.

Childhood friend, Emma, with me at 50th High School Reunion

Sunday school and church were important parts of our lives. Grandpa held a couple of positions at our church. I remember our church would have a week-long revival once a year, and the children who were not members of the church were seated on a mourner's bench while the preacher preached about hell and salvation. I remember when I was about eight years old, I made the decision that I wanted to be saved, because even at that age I recognized that something was missing in my life. I didn't know exactly what was wrong, but I knew that something was off. I was unhappy, and I wanted a better life. I also didn't want to take a chance on going to the fiery hell that the preacher preached about. Burning in brimstone and hellfire did not sound appealing. If it were salvation that I needed in order to feel better about myself and to avoid the brimstone and hellfire, then salvation it would be.

Someone told me that I needed to pray and ask God for a sign, and then I would know if I were saved. I can't remember clearly if it had been one of my parents, the preacher or who it was that said it, but I took the advice. I would frequently go outside of the house and pray, always asking God to save my soul and, in turn, promising to serve Him all the days of my life. I think I must've heard someone say that as well because I had no clue what salvation meant, nor did I know what it meant to serve Him at that time. I had no idea that my childish prayer was an oath. Neither did I know the severity of making an oath, a promise to God, and not keeping it.

I remember praying and asking God to show me a sign in the clouds if He had heard my prayers and saved my soul. I remember looking up and seeing the clouds form a shape that probably was just natural movement of the clouds, but I convinced myself that was my sign indicating God had heard my prayers, and I was now saved. My uncle joined the church that week, and so did I. We did everything together, and there was no way that I was going to let him leave me on that mourner's bench. We were baptized in a pond that was located a short distance behind the church. Getting baptized did not change the way I felt about myself, but it did seem to make my parents and grandparents proud, and that was enough for me at the time. I was learning early in life that my thoughts and feelings were not important, and this was yet another obstacle that I would have to overcome in the future. Church and school provided the greatest opportunities for me to gain attention.

When I did well in either place, it was always a topic for discussion, and that made me feel good to know I was pleasing my family. I was beginning to connect my self-worth to pleasing people. It's amazing how many residuals of abuse were presenting in my life at such an early age.

I enjoyed school and had an insatiable appetite for knowledge. Most of my early school memories were very pleasant. I can vividly remember, however, one early traumatic event that happened when I was about seven or eight years old. It was during school dismissal one afternoon. That memory haunted my thoughts for some time. We left school that day and were crossing the highway running from oncoming traffic as we had done so many times before. Suddenly one of the students panicked as she saw a car quickly approaching. She turned and attempted to run back in the opposite direction and was struck by the car. I still remember the image of her tiny body as it sailed through the air and landed on the side of the highway. That was a horrifying experience for all of us. It was a miracle that she survived. I remember seeing a massive lump on her forehead that probably resulted from her head hitting the pavement when she fell to the ground. She was taken away to the hospital as we looked on in a panic. After some time, she recovered, and we were all happy to see her return to school. Crossing the highway became a source of anxiety for me after that incident. I never forgot her accident, and how frightening it was to see that car strike her small body.

Even though that experience was extremely frightening, and I experienced flash backs of the event, I believe God protected my mind, because I did not suffer any lasting trauma residuals that interfered with my ability to learn.

Early trauma experiences can alter a child's brain chemistry and affect their ability to process and retain information. Thankfully, that was not the case with me. That incidence was yet another broken rung on my life's ladder that I am convinced God was helping me to climb.

I had experienced abuse early in life, physical and emotional, witnessed an accident where I thought a student would lose her life, and my ability to retain information had not been affected as could very well have been the case. I continued to thrive academically at the one-room church school.

I had heard a conversation between the grown-ups in the family about the possibility of moving to another plantation. Their conversation finally became a reality, and fourth grade would be my last year at the church school.

It was a sad day when the time finally came for us to move. It broke my heart to leave my school and the one best friend that I had made. It was a very emotional day for me. I was sad and teary. I didn't understand why it was necessary to move. I did not want to go. I loved my teacher. I would miss my friend. I did not want to start over in a strange place where I knew no one. I was shy and did not like to be in environments where I knew no one. I had become comfortable and felt secure in my school. But all of that was about to change. I was thinking as a child and only from my selfish childish perspective.

We were moving to another plantation because my father thought he would be better able to provide for his family. My grandparents were moving, too. At least I would have my uncle nearby, and I would not be totally alone. Little did I know the extent of how that move would change my life. My grandparents had always lived close to me. I spent much of my time at their house with my uncles and aunts. They were like brothers and sisters. We were one big family. Some people who remember us as children do not know that I am a niece, even today they think that my aunts and uncles are my sisters and brothers.

Now things were going to change with the move to the new plantation. Even though they were moving, they were not moving next door. They were not close enough for me to visit them alone as had been my pattern in the past. After that move, whenever I got to visit my grandparents, my parents had to take me. That limited my time with them. The move also resulted in more work for our little family. In the past, the family had worked together doing the field work. Moving to the new plantation changed the way they had worked prior. My grandparents went to one plantation, and my parents went to another. Therefore, they were no longer able to share the workload. My parents had their own plot of land to be responsible for and, now that I was nine years old, I was expected to help in the field all day long chopping or picking cotton alongside my parents, which was very new and challenging for me. I missed seeing my grandparents every day, especially Grandpa, and I missed playing with my uncle as well. Our relationship began to change. He too had to help my grandparents in the fields all day. As we grew older, our lives were more about hard work and very little play.

My Story
PART III

**Trust in the Lord with all your heart, and lean
not on your own understanding;
—Proverbs 3:5 (NKJV)**

Every little girl has her dreams, and I was no different in terms of dreaming. My dream was always about having a better life. I imagined myself living in a big beautiful home with glamorous things like those I saw in the magazines that I spent much of my free time looking at. I remember imagining myself lounging on one of the lovely couches that I saw in one of those old magazines, wearing a beautiful dress and sipping on a tall, fancy glass filled with iced tea. I spent most of the time as we worked, what seemed like endless hours in the blazing hot sun, dreaming of a better life. The cotton fields seemed to spark my motivation in terms of thinking how my life would be different when I grew up. I hated working in the fields with a passion and continually dreamed of the time when I would grow up and be away from that type of life and work. I would rescue my Momma from it as well.

Life was hard as the child of a sharecropper. We often had to get by with limited necessities of life. I can remember how my mother made many meals with only flour, salt, pepper, lard, salted pork, water, and baking powder. She would fry the salted pork, make biscuits and a white gravy that she called "tap gravy."

It looked very much like the country gravy that is served at some restaurants. Our meals were not very nutritious, but they served the purpose of preventing starvation.

As sharecroppers, we had to work for the entire year, and at the end of harvest time, there would be a meeting between my father and the landowner that Daddy called "settling-up time." My father was often informed at those meetings that he had incurred more debt than we had earned money to pay.

I never understood the concept of what was referred to as "sharecropping." In my mind, if we were sharing in the crops, we should also have been sharing in the money earned from them, but that was not the case. We rarely earned any money. We planted and grew most of our food. Momma learned to can fresh fruits and vegetables for winter months. We lived in a little shanty—this one had three rooms—but was still barely fit for human dwelling, and we worked from sun-up to sun-down, sometimes six days a week. Why there was such an exorbitant amount of debt incurred was always a mystery for me. I knew that during the winter months, my father took a small loan—usually two-hundred-dollars or less—from the landowner. It was just enough to buy some food staples that they had not been able to grow and preserve as well as to purchase a few clothing necessities for my return to school. After approximately four months, we were working again. It was very hard to understand how my father could incur so much debt.

From those early experiences, I learned some very valuable life lessons in survival that I have carried with me to this day. I learned early in life to be a good steward over that with which God blesses me. In addition, I learned to live within my means, trust God and be thankful for whatever gifts He provides. Whether gifts are tangible or spiritual, I learned from my childhood experiences that they were to be cherished and used wisely.

Our meals were usually not lavish at all; however, we never ate a meal without first giving thanks. Grandpa's father was a minister and had raised him to value prayer. Apparently, he had passed that value along to my father and mother, who in turn passed it along to me. We never ate a meal or went to bed without first saying a prayer. Even though I did not, at that time, understand the true value in prayer, I always said a prayer before meals and at bedtime.

My new school was different. It was not the intimate one-room church school that I had known, even though a couple of the teachers were familiar. The new school had students from the entire area that were bused to the school. It appeared large in comparison to the one-room church school, nevertheless there were only about four or five individual classrooms, with two classes in each room. The school had a large room with a stage that was used for school programs. I think that room was also used for classes because our programs were always at night. I was assigned to a wonderful teacher. She was slightly over four feet tall; however, this lady was a no-nonsense person. She was fair, compassionate, and demonstrated a genuine concern for each of her students personally as well as educationally. I remember that she kept a large switch at her desk, and she did not hesitate to use it whenever one of the students misbehaved. I was respectful, did my work, and we got along very well. She never used the switch on me and turned out to be one of my favorite teachers. I remember my last conversation with her. It was shortly after the purchase of our first home. I reached out to let her know what my life was like as an adult and mother. We had a wonderful conversation. I was ecstatically happy she still remembered me after such a long time.

As a child I remember always feeling as though I never quite belonged with most other children. I often felt like I didn't have much in common with girls my age.

I did not know what it was that made me different from all the other little girls. I was too young to understand that I had been set apart for the Lord's use, and even at a tender, young age, He was preparing me to do His work. I did not understand what it meant to be sanctified, set aside for the Lord's work. All I knew at that time was that I never felt like I fit in with the crowd. It was as if I was on the outside looking in most of the time. I was never the ordinary happy, carefree young girl, but continuously felt the need to be responsible, always eager to help someone in need when not pre-occupied with my thoughts and dreams. I had an old soul in a youthful body.

I remember those painful feelings of extreme aloneness that seemed to plague me almost constantly. Since I was an only child, maybe that contributed to some of those intense lonely feelings. My father was overprotective and extremely controlling. He did not allow me to venture out from the sight of either himself or my mother unless I was in the protective custody of some other family member. His over-protectiveness, coupled with the fact that I already felt like I did not fit in with other girls my age, may have impacted my ability to make friends. Of course, I did not have many friends.

I had started school early and was usually the youngest in my class. I remember the one-room church school as if it were yesterday. One room, two teachers, and several classes. This may have been the first open-space school concept. I still don't know how they managed it, but the two of them, principal and teacher, managed several grades very successfully. That experience became only a memory. The time had come to merge into another school with new experiences.

I remember the entrance to the school was through a hallway that was also used for hanging our coats. There were several boys that would wait for girls to enter the hallway after lunch and recess, jump from behind the hanging coats, grab, grope, and force kisses on them.

The boys thought it was funny, but it was emotionally upsetting for me and perhaps for some of the other girls as well. I don't know how the experience impacted them because we never spoke about it. Each of us carried our shame and humiliation in silence. I was only nine years old at the time but remember each incident vividly. There was always a level of anxiety when I entered that hallway because I was one of the targeted girls to be groped and kissed. Who would think that one would have experienced such a level of sexual harassment as early as middle school during that era? Sexual harassment is not a new phenomenon. It has been alive and well for quite some time. *"There is nothing new under the sun."* — *Ecclesiastes 1:9*

Here again I was experiencing feelings that I was destined to help others work through in the future. That early sexual harassment that I experienced at the new school was hands on training—no pun intended—for a greater purpose. Those feelings of helplessness, shame, and anxiety resulting from the hands of boys who had no idea that they were causing emotional trauma, were going to be useful in my future work. I believe that my past experiences enabled me to empathize with my clients in a unique way during my career as a therapist. When working with individuals suffering from residuals of sexual mishandling, I was able to relate to clients and establish a meaningful rapport in record time. There was purpose for each of my painful experiences that I believe God used for a greater purpose.

Even though there were aspects of the new school that I did not like, over all I loved school. I also loved church. I submerged myself in both school and church because the activities gave me an outlet and a means of gaining attention. I participated in every school play and church program, singing solos and reciting poems even though I would be literally shaking from anxiety. I always pushed past my fear and performed in a manner that consistently made my parents and grandparents proud. I was usually given leading roles in school plays because I could remember long lines. I was in love with school and learning.

This brought me comfort and a feeling of belonging because I could escape my reality and connect with a fantasy life in the pages of my books. I think I enjoyed being in the school plays because it gave me a sense of value. They needed me for the longer parts, and it felt good to be needed. I was getting the attention needed to feed my emotional hunger.

As I look back on those memories, I am convinced that the Lord was shaping my life for ministry, because I would someday teach others that it is possible to push past fears, anxieties, and other debilitating emotions to reach a place that exudes calm, peace, and tranquility through a relationship with Christ. That season in my life was a time of preparation for the ministry that I feel certain that God was calling me to do—healing the hurt from broken hearts.

My Story
PART IV

**And my God shall supply all your needs according
to his riches in glory by Christ Jesus.
—Philippians 4:19 (NKJV)**

M y family had very little money, and as a result we had very little reading materials in the home, but whatever book, magazine, or old newspaper that I could get my hands on, I read. We worked the field that was assigned to our family Monday through Friday. On some Saturdays, we had the opportunity to work the plantation owner's field for spending cash. I can remember vividly how we frequently began working in the field around 6:00 a.m. on many Saturday mornings and worked approximately ten hours only to be paid two dollars at the end of the day. With our cash—we were always paid in cash—we would purchase a few treat items to enjoy. I was always happy to earn my spending money, because I got a chance to keep all of it and spend it any way I chose, unless my father borrowed it, as he did frequently. He drove a tractor much of the time for which he was paid a small amount of cash weekly. His job was to spray insecticide on the cotton plants. When he was not helping my mother and me chop weeds from the cotton field, he was driving the tractor. From his small earnings, he shared with my mother for household necessities and always paid his debt to me, but sometimes only to borrow it back again later during the week. I think that was his way of teaching me to always pay my debts. He may have been immature in terms of parenting but taught me some valuable lessons about life.

My mother taught me to save, which was another important life lesson that has served me well. Whenever I had an opportunity to go with my parents into town on Saturday evenings after earning my spending cash, I usually purchased a piece of ribbon for my hair. I could get a half yard for five cents. I would usually purchase two yards of fabric for a new dress that my mother or grandmother would make for me. My grandmother was a talented dressmaker. She could look at a dress in the Sears catalog and make one identical without a pattern. She taught my mother the art of dressmaking as well. Between the two of them I must've been one of the best dressed girls in the community. I remember purchasing fabric that cost only fifty cents a yard, and I always purchased a little story book for twenty-five cents. I learned to budget well. I always saved enough for an ice cream, cookie, or a soda treat, Sunday school offering the next day, and a little for my piggy bank. Momma had a saying, "Always save something for a rainy day." I never forgot those words of wisdom. I learned some of my most meaningful life lessons from Momma.

I would sit for what seemed liked hours on Sunday afternoons under that big old oak tree at the edge of our little well-swept dirt yard where the ground seemed too hard for the grass to grow, outside that little three-room shack that we called home, reading and dreaming. I was a good reader and an even better dreamer.

As I sat under that tree, I would say to myself, "One day, I will be somebody!" I didn't realize that I was already somebody special in the eyes of God, and that He had purpose for the position that I was in. That is what happens when our self-esteem has been damaged. We fail to recognize our worth, and we attach our value to people and things. When we make those unhealthy attachments, they create a vulnerability to disappointments, frustrations, and feelings of failure.

In my ignorance of God's plan, coupled with low self-esteem, I subconsciously and sometimes consciously sought out reasons why I shouldn't like myself, and why others should not like me either. It was all in my mind of course. I frequently engaged in mental conversation with myself and was successful in convincing myself that I was too skinny, my hair was not long enough, my freckles made me ugly, and my list of negative self-talk went on and on. I had not learned to set my affections on things above as indicated in Colossians 3:2. As a child, my affections were set on how I appeared to others. My way of thinking was a perfect set-up for more heartache and disappointment.

I was just a mere child. Nonetheless, I am thoroughly convinced that God was preparing me for His purpose as I experienced many of the feelings that I would one day help others to manage. I was climbing my ladder, even with its broken rungs, and would learn later on as I matured that hardships in life are not designed to destroy us, but rather to strengthen and develop our character. I have grown to believe that life is neither good nor bad, it is all in how we perceive our experiences that we label it either good or bad. There is a lesson to be learned from every situation in life, thus giving each experience an option to be purposeful and enriching. It is my opinion that the quality of each experience is determined by our perception.

Middle school was memorable in several ways. One of which was that I was forced to interact with many new students, and I experienced a level of sexual harassment. But not all middle school memories were unpleasant. One of my most pleasant memories of middle school occurred during the winter of my sixth-grade year, when a new student was assigned to my classroom. He was polite, and very handsome. He did not take part in harassing the girls in the hallway as some of the other boys were doing. He was quiet and appeared somewhat shy. He started school in the middle of the year because his family had just moved into the community.

His seat was on the opposite side of the classroom, because he was not in my class. Our teacher taught fifth and sixth grades in the same room. The new student was a good basketball player. He and a group of boys played each day during recess. The girls gathered near the basketball court to watch the game and flirt with the boys. I have never been a basketball fan, but I gathered near the court with the other girls to watch. I was not at all interested in the game, but I was most definitely interested in this new student. I was only ten years old, and if my father had known I was interested in a boy, that would have caused a major problem for me. I knew I had to keep my interest in this boy to myself.

Occasionally, he and I would exchange a look or a smile. After some time, we gained the courage to exchange a word here and there. I was shy, but this new boy was even more shy than I was. When the boys left the court, he always made it a point to walk around the side of the court where I was sitting. Our eyes would always meet, and we would both share a nervous smile. It took some time before we got up enough courage to speak to each other.

I believe that God was continually working His plan for my life. Who would have ever imagined that extremely shy, handsome boy would someday become my husband? I'm thoroughly convinced that God was putting the pieces of my life together like a puzzle. Every piece fitting perfectly in place for His glory.

My dreams for a better life were not only for myself. I also dreamed of making a better life for my mother. Momma and I had a unique relationship. Even though I knew she was my mother and never disrespected her position as such, there was a closeness between us more like girlfriends. Perhaps that was because we were so close in age or maybe it was because we only had each other for companionship most of the time. Whatever the reason, Momma was my best friend, and I was hers.

It broke my heart to see how hard she worked in the field. After long hot hours in the sun chopping or picking cotton, I watched my dear sweet mother come home, make a fire in that wood-burning stove, and create a meal from what seemed like nothing at all useful. She washed the family's clothes by hand using a #2 tub and washboard. I helped as much as possible, but my mother did the bulk of the work. I dreamed of a day when I could help her enjoy a better life. I thought that if anyone deserved better, it would have to be my sweet mother.

My desire to help extended beyond family. I was drawn to anyone who was hurting physically or emotionally. I did not understand it then, but I came to realize that was the hand of God leading me in the direction He was calling me to serve. Every experience I had was useful in shaping me into a vessel to be used by Him for the specific purpose of facilitating healing for emotionally hurting individuals.

I did not know then that my mission in life would be to help heal the hurt of those suffering from emotional pain. All I could understand at that time in my life and for many years to come, was that I felt incomplete, disconnected from most people and sometimes even from family. I could never quite fit in with the activities that my peers involved themselves in that they seemed to have derived enjoyment from. Oh yes, I tried it for a season, but my season was short lived.

That happens when one has been sanctified, set apart for the Lord's work. It was not His purpose for me to become comfortable with the ways of the world. He is a jealous God.

Eighth grade appeared to come and go quickly, soon it was time for graduation and the transition to high school. I remember my eighth-grade graduation. Momma took me shopping to purchase material for a new dress and my first pair of high-heeled shoes. I don't remember the dress, but I remember the shoes. They were black medium heels with a bow on the back, and they did not fit my feet well at all. I was so excited to get my first pair of high heels that I was not concerned with the proper fit. The shoes were much too large. By the end of graduation day, I had the most painful blisters one could ever imagine on the back of both feet that had resulted from the shoes rubbing against my heels. It took several days for my feet to begin healing from the damage caused by those shoes sliding up and down on my feet. The scars from those blisters remained for a very long time. Eighth-grade graduation was most definitely a memorable time.

PART V

And we know that all things work together for good to those who love God, to those who are the called according to His purpose
— Romans 8:28 (NKJV)

H igh school was both exciting and scary. Exciting because my friend from the church school was now at the high school, and we were inseparable once again. Scary because it was enormous when compared with middle school. It was a challenge finding my way around the campus. It appeared massive, and there were so many students. Buses came from miles away bringing students from several different communities to the school. We changed rooms for every class and had a different teacher for each one. That was a huge change, and it was challenging finding my classes and getting to them on time. When I got the hang of things, I settled in and became more comfortable with the work experience, but not so much the high school experience.

As I observed other students who appeared to have such fulfilled and happy lives, I began to wonder again, "What is wrong with me?" I wondered why I could not have the fun-filled life that I thought others were enjoying. I didn't understand why life appeared to be so difficult for me. I know now that it was because my ladder had many broken rungs making it more difficult to climb.

Because of my painful experiences, I was left with a tremendous amount of emotional baggage that needed to be unpacked. I was in constant conflict with myself, and my negative self-talk was almost constantly occurring.

I was not allowed to attend school functions like many of the other girls. I admired those girls who ran for Homecoming Queen. They looked so beautiful and were the popular girls around campus. I did my work and kept a low profile on campus because I never felt good enough to associate with the "pretty" girls. I did not feel like I belonged with such a popular group of girls. Their parents were not sharecroppers like mine were. Many of their parents owned their own land and homes, and in my mind, the girls flaunted that fact with their attitudes.

As I think back on those feelings, I am almost certain I created the image that I wanted to see in my own mind because my self-esteem was so damaged. I probably looked for ways to isolate myself, either out of my fear of rejection or from the embarrassment of knowing that Daddy was so controlling. I would never be able to participate in extracurricular activities that would require me to be out of the house at night.

I grew up in poverty. I shared the work with my parents on a farm. I had to work long hours in the fields to help support myself and the family. Working the fields was torture for me because I had an extreme fear of worms. I think I was more afraid of worms than snakes. At least the snakes would run away if they heard me coming. The plush green leaves of the cotton plants were breeding ground for all types of the little squiggly critters, and I remained in a state of continual stress and anxiety when working in the field.

It was difficult to determine what caused more stress—the worms everywhere or my father's yelling and harsh words. He did not have much patience and knew absolutely nothing about parenting skills. His idea of good parenting was to make sure that my needs were met in terms of food, shelter, and clothes. That cotton was what he thought was a means to that end.

A vast majority of children born to teen parents spend their early years in poverty. At that point in my life, I was right on target with regard to where statistics suggested I would be in terms of living in poverty. Statistics further indicated that being born to teen parents put me in a category of children who were unlikely to finish high school, to be at greater risk of socio-emotional problems, and with a greater probability of starting my own family at an early age. Economically, my life began statistically on point. I started life in poverty. I experienced some social and emotional issues, but that was not the intended plan God had in mind for the duration of my lifespan. Those other statistical indicators were not consistent. I beat the odds. It is my belief that God protected me because He had selected me for a greater purpose. Statistics and circumstances were not designed to define my life. I further believe that God defined and designed my life even before conception, because He had a plan for me and was preparing me according to His blueprint.

I remember one day being in a panic as I worked in the field. I had spotted what appeared to me as gigantic worms on the cotton leaves near me and began to scream with fear. Instead of my father, the one who any young girl would think of as their protector, rushing to rescue and comforting me, his remarks were, "Stop looking for them and you won't find them!" That memory resonated in my mind for years to come. I have never been able to forget that day, nor have I been able to forget how I felt when I heard his words. Parents can cause tremendous emotional damage to their children and never even realize it.

My Grandpa would never have responded to me that way. He had a gentler personality and was always kind, patient, and loving with me. I always felt safe with him.

My father's response was probably due to his lack of parental skills, since he had been a teen parent. During that era, there were no parenting classes to teach young parents the appropriate way to interact with their children to promote healthy emotional growth. He most likely thought his remarks would be helpful to me in some way. Instead, they were painful beyond description and emotionally damaging.

His remarks appeared to me at that time as a lack of concern for my safety and well-being. It hurts to the core when the person that is expected to protect you appears not to be concerned about you. That creates feelings of insecurity, anxiety, and helplessness which in many instances can result in emotional anguish.

Life for me was no *cake-walk*. I began working the fields from the tender age of nine. The days were long, hot, and frightening. I had to endure the torture of fieldwork from spring until late fall. I still remember the corn in my hands from the handle of the hoe rubbing against them when chopping cotton. The corn would last the entire spring to summer and then came the torn cuticles on my fingers as a result of picking cotton from fall to winter. The cotton bulbs opened in sections and each section had a sharp point at the end of the bulb. My fingers often got cut by one of the sharp edges as I clumsily attempted to pull the cotton from the bulb.

School attendance for me was always sporadic during the first month. I was only able to attend school if it rained and the fields were too wet to work. After the first month, however, my father made sure that I went to school at least four days out of each week.

Whatever needed to be done in the fields, I would help on Fridays, after school or on the weekend. My father had an agreement with the owner of the farm, and it was understood between them that after a certain number of days, I would attend school. They additionally had an understanding that he was not to personally address me or my mother about work or anything else. Any directions for me or my mother were to be directed to Daddy, and he would pass the word to his family. That was his way of being in charge of his home. I never figured out if he was being protective or controlling. Either way that worked in our favor. As I reflect on it, I believe he was being protective of what he saw as his belongings, and his control was his way of showing how much he treasured us.

My father had the reputation of being *crazy* so no one, black or white, wanted to cross him. There was talk that he had never been the same after returning home from the war. I can now see his idiosyncrasy as favor in terms of orchestrating a means for getting me into school. While many of the neighborhood children were still working the fields as per the landowner's directions, I was in school getting my education, thanks to Daddy.

Even though I got a late start in school each year, God blessed me. I worked hard and excelled. Here again, I beat the odds that were against me. I climbed despite the broken rungs. A child of teen parents will often have a low IQ and low academic achievement. That was not my story. I was always in the top percentile of my classes even after getting a late start and playing catch-up. I loved learning. Books were my escape from current reality, but most of all, I think God was showing me His favor. He was teaching me how to climb above problematic circumstances and how to do it gracefully. I was learning a lesson that I would later teach to others. *Our circumstances do not define us!*

Even though ours was a small family of only three, there was never enough money for the family to have everything that we needed or desired. God blessed my mother with magnificent gifts. Even though she was very young, she was an incredibly resourceful and creative young woman. It seemed as if she could take nothing and make something out of it. Her favorite quote was, *"Take what you have, and make what you want."* I live by her philosophy and have passed it down to my children and grandchildren as our family mantra.

I admired my mother. I watched her take little and transform it into much many times throughout my childhood. The family did not go hungry. There was always something that my mother could use and miraculously create a tasty meal. Daddy would go hunting and bring home a rabbit, squirrel, or some other wild game. He would dress his kill, and Momma would work her magic in the kitchen. I remember one of my favorite Saturday afternoon treats was when Momma made her special tomato sandwiches. She used fresh tomatoes from the garden, salt, pepper, and mayonnaise. I never outgrew my love for those sandwiches. I remember going out to lunch with friends a few years ago. I ordered a BLT and asked the waiter to hold the bacon. He looked somewhat surprised but returned with my tomato sandwich. It did not taste the same as Momma's, but was enjoyable, nonetheless.

The kitchen was not the only place that I saw my mother take what she had and make what she wanted. One of my most vivid memories of Momma taking what she had to make what she wanted was when I reached dating age, and Daddy finally gave his consent for me to have a boyfriend. She wanted to create a space for my friend to sit and socialize when he came to visit. We did not have money for a sofa, so Momma made a settee out of an old, discarded car seat. That car-seat-turned-settee was in the family until I went off to college. God always provided for our needs. We may not have had anything fancy, but our needs were always provided for.

My ladder to the good life was damaged; however, the broken rungs would not prevent my climb. By the grace of God, even though I did not recognize it at the time, I was defying the odds and setting a record of family firsts. I would be the first in the family to complete high school. I was to be the first in the family to earn a college degree, and the first in the family to earn an advanced degree. Although my parents did not have a high school education, they always encouraged me toward education as the way to a better life. I trusted them and worked as hard as I could to get that education—they told me would provide the better life which I so desperately desired.

Daddy's military experience had afforded him the opportunity to see a different side of life. He observed the difference education could make in the quality of one's life during his travels. He told me that education was my way to a better life, and he and Momma did what they could to make that happen for me. I was very fortunate that my parents had that level of insight. At a time when most people we knew seemed to have been focused on merely surviving, my mom and dad were focused on surviving and thriving.

When I completed high school and decided I wanted to go to college, it created quite a discussion in the family. Where would the money for tuition come from? There was not a high school counselor at my school to advise me in terms of loans, scholarships, or work-study programs. The family would have to come up with the money to pay for college. Even though tuition was only approximately seventy-five dollars per semester, that figure sounded like a small fortune to my family who were poor sharecroppers living in poverty in the 60's.

One of my aunts suggested that my parents forget about college and send me to the city where I could find myself a job to make some money. Two of my aunts and an uncle were already living in the city. She further stated that I did not need to go to college because I would only get pregnant, embarrass the family, and make my parents cry from broken hearts, as if the same behavior couldn't have happened in the city. I did not understand her rationale but kept quiet and let the adults work out the solution. Distractions will come, but the will of God always prevails! His purpose for me was working even though I had no idea. I remember talking to my parents about what I wanted to be. I wanted to have a title, those fancy letters, after my name. I thought that such a title would prove my worth. God allowed me to eventually acquire the title, but it was not to prove my worth. Instead, that title was meant to do His work.

My parents were proud and excited about the idea of my going to college because they had always encouraged me to get my education. Neither of them had been able to acquire an education beyond middle school, yet they saw the value in education and wanted that advantage for their daughter. They found pleasure in my achievements and wanted to give me those things they did not realize were possible for themselves. I was an only child at that time, and I think they saw me as somewhat of an extension of themselves and vicariously shared in my educational success.

The conversation was ongoing in terms of college or the city. Yes, I had been the first to graduate from high school. That was a milestone for the family, but college would be an even greater achievement. A college education would surely offer me the better life that my parents and I envisioned. It would reveal a whole new world, not just for me but for my family as well. Daddy's travel while in the military had afforded him the opportunity to see more of the world than anyone else in the family had been privileged to see.

He had observed the difference in terms of how those that were educated lived in comparison to the uneducated. He was keenly aware of the difference in their quality of life. Daddy wanted that improved quality of life for his little girl. He wasn't a patient man, he wasn't gentle, and he had a foul mouth, but he wanted the very best that he could possibly provide for me. That was how he showed his love, by providing the best that he could for his family. He didn't know much about emotional security, but he did know the security of having a good job with a steady paycheck. That was what he wanted for his little girl.

The serious conversations seem to have always taken place at my grandparents' home. My Grandpa was the strong, quiet type. He was an introspective, Godly man, and very intelligent. He was an observer who didn't talk much, but when he did speak, he always made a valuable contribution to whatever was being discussed. He was a man of wisdom. I think everyone that knew him respected his opinion. He had that way of being the final authority on everything, so when Grandpa said, "If the girl wants to go to college, send her," that was the end of the discussion. It was as if my parents needed permission to do what they already knew they should and wanted to do in the first place. After Grandpa completed his short but powerful input into the conversation, Momma and Daddy went into action and began working out their game plan, because Grandpa had settled the discussion. I was going to college!

Age 17

That summer was a memorable one for me in more ways than one. The excitement of going to college in the fall was overshadowed by the sudden death of my beloved Grandpa. He did not get the opportunity to share the excitement that I was basking in as a result of the final life decision that he had helped to make for me.

Once a year, churches in the area hosted a revival meeting. The yearly church revivals were going on that week. One at the local church and the other one at our church. Grandpa loved his church. He had served in ministry there for as long as I could remember.

The family did not own a car, so he walked to the church as he had done many times before. After working in the field and enduring the sweltering heat all day, he came home, cleaned himself up, and left home walking to his church. The walk to church was not something unusual. He did it frequently. Sometimes he would start out walking, someone would pick him up and give him a ride, and other times I think he walked the entire distance. The walk that evening was to be his final journey.

The church was several miles away and at the top of a steep hill. It was the same church where I had attended school eight years prior. Grandpa must have exerted too much energy walking to the church in the hot summer sun because, soon after his arrival, he collapsed. We were informed later that evening by a doctor at the hospital that he had suffered a cerebral hemorrhage. One of the church deacons owned a pickup truck. Grandpa was placed in the back of his truck and driven to the hospital. It was approximately eight miles away from the church. I'm sure the rough ride was not a good idea but there was no alternative. Poor people during that time did not have access to paramedics, neither was there a telephone available to call even if paramedics had been a possibility. Apparently, the deacon did not arrive at the hospital in time, because the doctors were not able to revive Grandpa. He expired shortly after arriving at the hospital.

My parents and I had attended the revival at the local church that evening. We were walking back home when a truck came speeding down the road. We all stepped to the side to allow the truck to pass. It was pitch dark and we were unable to recognize the truck at first. However, it did not pass us as we had anticipated. The driver was looking for my father to give him the news that Grandpa had been rushed to the hospital. In a panic, we made our way to the hospital and shortly thereafter received word that Grandpa did not make it. He was dead.

I felt as though something inside of me died along with the news that grandpa was dead. He had been my spiritual role model. He was a man of the word who took his relationship with the Lord seriously. I loved him with all my heart. My Grandpa had always been there as my rock. He was the first man I had ever loved, the first man I had ever bonded with. What would my life be like without him? What would I do without his wisdom? I loved him with every fiber of my being, and I was sure he loved me just as much. What would I do without his loving protection? My poor heart was breaking. I was an emotional wreck. I didn't think I would ever be able to stop crying. It felt as if there was a gaping hole in my heart from which I could literally feel my blood slowly and continuously draining. That was pain like I had never experienced before. Grandpa had always been my consolation, my sense of security. Now he was gone. I felt alone, vulnerable, exposed, and helpless to help myself. I recall crying for days. I was unable to sleep, and I lost my appetite as well. I remember Daddy telling me, "You have to eat, or you will die too." I had battled low mood, off and on for some time. I think this was a case of full-blown depression.

That shy little boy who had entered my sixth-grade classroom approximately six years prior, the very one who I pretended to watch play basketball at recess every day, was now a handsome young man. He was extremely supportive and loving during my time of grief. It turned out that he had been as much into me as I had been into him. He was now my boyfriend and would later become my husband. Norris stepped up as my strongest support person and was by my side helping me and my family through the entire grieving period and beyond. He was amazing.

His father had purchased a car, and he was the designated driver. His father had told him that, because he was so responsible, the car was his. Since my family did not own a car, Norris graciously used his car to provide transportation for the family as arrangements were made for Grandpa's funeral. He's not only provided transportation but, in addition, provided a strong shoulder of support for me to lean on during those times when my grief appeared to be unbearable. He had enjoyed a relationship with my grandpa as well. Norris had solicited Grandpa's assistance several times when he ran into trouble with math assignments. My Grandpa had been his tutor.

Grandpa had a good education for one born during his era (1900). I learned later that his father was also able to read and write. According to the 1910 US Federal Census, Grandpa's father was listed as a Mulatto, able to read and write. His occupation, to my surprise, was not listed as a farmer, but as Clergy. That explained why Grandpa valued education and had such a reverence for God. Both apparently had been esteemed in his home as he grew up. I don't think there was anyone in the community who did not love and respect my grandpa. He was my hero, for sure, and was going to be missed by many in various ways.

The funeral was traumatic for me. The image of him lying in front of the little church, a place I had once loved so much, in his casket still resonates in my memory. Daddy had told me that if I touched his body that would help me get over the pain of losing him. Perhaps he thought touching him would somehow help me come to terms with the fact that he was gone and was going to bring closure for me. I was so distraught that I was willing to try anything that was suggested if it meant easing my pain. I remember touching his face. His face did not feel like my grandpa, but instead it was cold, hard, and lifeless. It felt more like the bark on a dead tree. I had never touched a dead body before, so I had no idea what to expect. I felt a little shocked, confused, and frightened, but the pain of Grandpa being dead and in that casket trumped every other feeling that I was experiencing. Touching his body did not serve the intended purpose of bringing closure to my pain. It was an extremely difficult experience, but we got through the funeral.

Several weeks passed. We had to pick up the pieces and go on with our lives. After all, that is what Grandpa probably would have told us to do in no uncertain terms. Soon, the time came to resume our game plan regarding college. Grandpa had already settled the debate before he died, and it was understood by all that I would be going to college in the fall. I had been accepted and was on my way to Mississippi Vocational College to pursue a degree in Business Education. I was attempting to think pro-actively with my degree choice. I thought a degree in business would provide a wider range of job opportunities. I could teach or work in the corporate arena.

Instead of sending me to the city to find a job, as my aunt had suggested, my parents decided they would go instead and find jobs, because my education was important to them and had been important to Grandpa. They sold what they could sell and gave away other items that were in the home before packing their clothes and taking a bus to the city. My parents moved in with one of my aunts. They both found jobs working at a hotel.

Daddy and Momma at work

Since neither of them had graduated high school, they were limited in the type of work they could find. It did not matter to them that they cleaned hotel rooms for a living. It was a job and paid them a steady salary. They worked hard, saved their money, and were soon able to move into their own apartment. My parents were accustomed to working hard, but now they were getting better wages for their hard work, and they paid my college expenses proudly. It made them happy that their daughter was going to college. In that day, a college education was an enormous achievement. Not many in our circles could boast of that accomplishment, and it made my parents proud that they could. They wanted to give me a better chance in life than what they thought was possible for themselves, and it was happening.

Grandpa's advice to send me to college turned out to be a win-win. The quality of life began to improve significantly for my parents, and I was on my way to a better life. In spite of horrendous obstacles, I was climbing the ladder in search of my destiny, even though many rungs had been broken.

Going off to college was a challenge for me. I was not prepared socially for the challenges that I was about to encounter as a college student. I could hold my own academically, but socially it was a different story.

I had lived an extremely sheltered life. My father had been overprotective and controlling. All major decisions had been made for me; therefore, I was not at all prepared to live on my own. In his mind, I think he probably assumed that his overprotectiveness and control were a means of protection from individuals who may have meant me harm. However, in some respects it was damaging because I did not learn how to make sound decisions for myself. I was somewhat of an introvert, overly sensitive, and had very low self-esteem. I found myself in uncomfortable situations frequently because

I did not have the needed social skills to maneuver through college life as an independent thinker. I was not secure enough with myself to make my own choices. Instead, I would normally go along with the choices of others simply because I wanted to fit in and hide the fact that I was naive. I kept quiet instead of speaking my mind in certain situations because of insecurity which gave a false sense of agreement and acceptance of others' behaviors. Instead of protecting me, I think that my father's parenting style left me more vulnerable to being misused and hurt.

Parents who are overly involved in their child's decision-making processes do them a great disservice. Children need to be taught how to make social decisions and be allowed to experience what success and failure feels like. They need to know that if a mistake is made, it is okay to restructure and start again with the loving support and encouragement of their parents.

I started drinking alcohol and smoking cigarettes because others were doing it, and I wanted to be accepted. So, I did what those that I considered popular students were doing. I finally had an opportunity to interact with others and was determined not to feel the same aloneness that I had felt as a child growing up on the farm. I gave in to peer pressure and made some very poor decisions that I am not proud of. I believe that God protected and kept me because He had a plan for my life. Although the enemy desired to destroy me, God's grace kept me.

My parents had modeled drinking and smoking for me early in life. They both smoked cigarettes and drank alcohol. I had watched them for as long as I could remember rolling their cigarettes with small sheets of white paper filled with smoking tobacco that they poured from small red containers. Momma drank beer, and Daddy drank whiskey and beer. He had learned to make a homemade beer that they called homebrew from a recipe that my mother's father had taught him.

He would make his homebrew, put it in empty soda bottles, and cap it. I guess that was something rather common to do at that time because he could find caps for his bottles and he had a special tool that secured the caps on the bottles. He knew when it was ripe to drink. Even though I was just a child, Daddy would always give me my special little bottle of his homebrew.

Most weekends, Daddy went out with his drinking buddies and came home drunk. Momma and I were always home, nervously awaiting his return, because we never knew what to expect when he arrived. Sometimes he would come home and go to sleep, and then there were other times when he would come home and start an argument with either my mother or me. When I was the target of his rant, the argument was always one-sided because I was not allowed to talk back to him.

He had a foul mouth. I got cursed out many times, whether he was drunk or sober. That was his choice of discipline. He controlled me with his harsh words. It would have been less painful to have suffered physical punishment than having endured the many years of verbal abuse. Daddy had no idea of the impact his harsh words were having on my psyche, nor how many years it would take me to heal from the emotional scars that resulted. Residual damage from emotional abuse has been found to last longer than that of any other form. Even though my emotions were damaged, they were not in a state of disrepair. That process represented another broken rung on my ladder that God would help me to climb.

My father's anger management issues may have resulted from trauma experienced during the war. There was not any information available to him regarding post war trauma. I remember he suffered from severe back pain and traveled a few times for treatments at a

Veteran's Hospital. I also remember some talk about *shell shock*. I remember him being super-sensitive to sudden loud noises. There were never any discussions in terms of the emotional impact of the war. Perhaps he did not even realize the emotional toll that horrific experience had taken on him. There was no counseling available to help him identify and process his feelings regarding the traumatic experiences of serving in the war.

Daddy could be sweet and kind one minute and a raging maniac the next. We did not realize his behavior could possibly have been PTSD.

I can remember an extremely frightening incident that occurred before Grandpa died. Daddy came home drunk one day and fell across the bed. We thought he was going to sleep it off, but instead he managed to fall out of the bed onto the floor. He jumped up apparently disoriented and accused me of throwing him onto the floor. He scrambled to his feet and grabbed his twelve-gauge shotgun from the rack that he had made on the wall over the bed to hold it. Then he went to the top drawer of the wardrobe where he kept the ammunition. He proceeded to call me some of his harshest words as he broke the gun down to load it. He was woozy from the alcohol and, therefore, his reflexes were off which gave Momma and me a chance to run out of the back door and hide in some nearby bushes.

He stumbled out of the house looking for us. We could hear him talking and laughing to himself as he searched for us. I remember hearing him say that we were running like scared little rabbits. We did not move until he was far enough away that we could no longer hear him. When we thought it was safe, we ran in the opposite direction and went to my grandparents house.

Later that evening when he had sobered up, Daddy came looking for us. He no longer had the shotgun and was talking as if nothing had happened. It was as if he did not remember the incident at all.

Even though he did not seem to remember what had taken place earlier in the day the memory remained with me. The distressing incident was another broken rung on the ladder that God was going to help me climb. Daddy continued to experience mood swings; however, there were no other events involving his gun.

PART VI

The Lord shall preserve you from all evil; he shall preserve your soul.
—Psalm 121:7 (NKJV)

The scars of childhood abuse affected the way I viewed myself and the world for many years. Abuse alters one's perceptions. I can remember how I often misunderstood the intentions of others. I set myself up to be taken advantage of in many social situations, simply because I misread the motives of individuals that I was associated with. I oscillated from being too trusting to looking for hidden agendas in almost every conversation I had with another person. I had learned early on in my life how to be a physical fighter, but emotionally I was wide open, defenseless, and vulnerable. I had no emotional boundaries. I had a sharp tongue, just like Daddy, yet quick to apologize if I thought I had hurt or disappointed someone even if that person had wronged me. I was in constant conflict with myself, and my inner confusion added to my stress level and emotional pain. I had learned from childhood experiences that my feelings weren't valued. I thought that I needed to prove myself worthy of attention, so I worked over-time at proving myself to others in the effort to acquire their acceptance.

I had extremely low self-esteem second guessing almost everything I did. It was difficult to make decisions, so, I frequently blended in with the actions of others which evidenced as a huge mistake while attempting to adjust to my new life as a college student. As I implied earlier, college was a challenge.

Before my parents moved to the city, they arranged for me to live in town so that I would be near the college bus route. They could not afford for me to live on campus. I rode the bus to class each day along with other students who lived off campus.

I had grown up having very little voice about anything—especially in terms of making major life choices—and now, at age seventeen, I was expected to live as an adult with the responsibility of having to make those verdicts for myself. I no longer had the luxury of Momma and Daddy or my grandpa interceding for me when it came to important decisions. Grandpa had made his transition from the earth, and Momma and Daddy had moved to another state which seemed like a world away. My grandmother was also miles away and unaware of anything that was going on with me.

I was a young country girl possessing virtually no social skills and who had been suddenly thrust into a culturally new and extremely challenging environment. That was a recipe for disaster and a situation ripe for more abuse to occur.

I was finally free to come and go with whomever I chose. This new freedom was totally the opposite of the life that I had been accustomed to living. I think I was given too much responsibility without proper training in terms of what to do with it. I attempted to grow up fast but had a tremendous struggle learning the healthiest way to do that. I was seventeen years old, but far from being a responsible adult. I had been treated like a child for seventeen years and now expected to magically know how to be an adult. Unfortunately, that is a mistake made by some parents even today.

As a result of my gross lack of skills in terms of navigating my way through the new life that I had been suddenly placed into, I found myself in several dicey situations.

I remember one situation that I encountered a young man who befriended me. He was several years older. I was flattered at first to have the attention of this older guy. Initially, our conversations were about school assignments that I was working on, but eventually our talks became more personal. I became somewhat uneasy with his visits but was conflicted and didn't quite know how to stop them. On one of his visits, he touched me inappropriately and attempted to kiss me. It was a struggle to fight him off. I was afraid to tell anyone about his behavior because I thought people would blame me. Somehow, when a girl was violated in those days, it was always thought to be her fault, and recent reports of sexual harassment have proven that not much is changed even today. Unfortunately, sexual abuse was usually considered to be the female's fault. The assumption being that she would have led him on in some manner, and I was afraid that if I told, I would be viewed in a negative way. In my mind, I was helpless. I felt that I had no other choice but to keep quiet and protect myself to the best of my ability. I suffered in silence. I felt all alone, without anyone to advocate for me.

There were many other snares designed to destroy me, but I believe God protected me because I was not destined to be just another unfortunate statistic. When I reflect on the direction that my life had taken up to that point in time, I see proof that He will preserve one from evil.

I continued my quest to find my space in the new life that I struggled to make sense of. I was somewhat of a follower for a time because I wanted so desperately to fit in with the girls who I perceived as popular. A poor self-image will cause one to make poor decisions and, during this time in my life, I was making a lot of extremely poor decisions.

I persisted in what was, in my opinion, social drinking, smoking, and some party-going—sometimes during school nights. There were many times when I had to complete assignments during the bus ride to campus because I had stayed out too late the night before and fell asleep while attempting to complete my homework. I was very insecure and wanted to be accepted so badly that whenever anyone invited me to a party, I would say yes even if I knew that I should've said no. I was desperately seeking acceptance even at the risk of blowing my chances for the much-coveted education I said I wanted and for which my parents were sacrificing to provide. It didn't take long before my grades reflected the lack of commitment to my education, and I earned a 'D' for the first time ever.

That 'D' frightened me. It was the wake-up call I needed to begin to put first things first. I knew that my parents would want to see copies of my grades, and my mother would be extremely disappointed in me. Just the thought of my mother being disappointed in me was somewhat sobering. I always wanted to make her proud. The sheer idea of Momma being disappointed made me rethink some of my behaviors. But on the other hand, my daddy would be furious. I was well aware that Daddy had anger management problems, and even though he was hundreds of miles away, I still feared his wrath. I could imagine him cussing me out in 'daddy fashion.' I remembered that vicious tongue and his way of using it often cutting me to my core.

Even though I was determined to live my life on as much of my own terms as possible, I knew I had to keep my grades up because of the sacrifice that Momma and Daddy were making for me to get an education. I had too much invested in me to blow my chances for success. I didn't stop partying and attempting to fit in with the popular girls. Nevertheless, I paid more attention to my grades.

Freshman year was my most difficult one. There were many adjustments that had to be made. I had to adjust to the horrible fact that my beloved Grandpa was gone, and I would never see him again or hear his gentle comforting voice. I had to adjust to being on my own playing the role of an adult, even though I was immature and very much a child. I needed to adjust to being separated from my parents who had been my major decision-makers. I had to adjust to sexual misconduct and innuendos from some of the young men who presented as friends. I also had to adjust to being manipulated by some associates I considered friends even though my grandmother had already identified them as *'dirty buddies.'* And let's not forget that college work was a lot more difficult than high school had been. Even though I graduated in the top percentile of my high school class, I was still virtually unprepared for much of my college work. I could regurgitate facts but never learned the art of critical thinking which contributed tremendously to my freshman year struggle in college.

At the end of freshman year, I got my chance to go to visit my parents in Chicago for the summer. That was an exciting time. It was wonderful to see my parents, aunts, and uncles. The bright lights of the big city were mesmerizing. I had visited a couple of smaller cities on occasion, but the lights in them did not compare to the lights in Chicago. It was always busy there, and the city appeared to be bright all night long. It was as though no one ever slept.

The Lounge was the place to be on Friday and Saturday nights. The owner was someone my father knew. The family patronized the establishment almost every weekend. The legal age to get in was twenty-one. I was only eighteen. Nonetheless, my uncle and Daddy would bring me with them, and no one questioned my age, perhaps because they knew the family.

My uncle introduced me to a new mixed drink called a screwdriver. It was made from a mixture of vodka and orange juice. Since the owner knew I was under age, I suspect my drink was probably more orange juice. We would drink and dance until the lounge closed. I did more dancing than drinking because I was afraid I would lose control if I consumed too much alcohol. People who have been abused often develop a strong need for control. I needed to be aware of everything that was happening; therefore, I couldn't afford to overdo the alcohol. I also remembered how Daddy behaved when he was under the influence, and I never wanted to take a chance on acting in such an embarrassing and hurtful manner.

My uncle was my dance partner. Occasionally, he would allow me to dance with his best friend who usually joined us at our table. Daddy trusted my uncle to pick me up in his car and take me to the lounge even if he were not going himself. I enjoyed my time in the big city. I found a summer job to help with my college expenses. My parents had instilled in me a strong work ethic, and I developed a need to take care of myself. I can remember them saying to me, "Learn how to take care of yourself so you don't have to depend on anyone to do it for you." Those words stayed with me, and I believe were instrumental in instilling a strong sense of independence which has served me well throughout my adulthood. They taught me to take initiative and not wait for others to do what I could do for myself.

With the monies I saved from my summer employment, I was able to purchase clothes for school. I felt good about that. It gave me a sense of independence. Working in the city was much more lucrative than working on the farm had been. City life was a new and exciting experience that had both positive and negative consequences.

Daddy had not changed much. He still had anger management issues. His temper appeared to have been even more explosive at times, because he had more access to alcohol, which seemed to always affect his behavior negatively. He often got into arguments with his brother over seemingly minor things. The family usually got together at my parents' apartment to play cards on weekends when not at the Lounge. There would be beer, whiskey, and soda to drink. Momma would make hot dogs or fry fish. We would eat, drink, and have fun playing cards and dancing to music until Daddy lost his temper over some trivial issue and started arguing. Usually with his brother or Momma. Life for me continued to be an emotional rollercoaster. His arguments were always extremely anxiety-provoking for me. I was rarely at ease in Daddy's presence and felt like I was walking on eggshells because I never knew what word or action would provoke his anger toward me.

The summer passed quickly, and it was time to return to college. I remember proudly packing my new clothes I had purchased with the money from my summer job into the suitcase and heading for the bus station to return to college. I felt sad to leave. Tears of sadness escaped my eyes as I looked out the window and saw matching ones roll down Momma's cheeks when I boarded the bus. Momma and I shared a special relationship and tears at separation became a routine that happened each time we parted.

It was a long, silent bus ride back. I reflected on my experience in the big city, thought about what sophomore year would be like, ate the food Momma had packed for my trip, and slept. After what seemed like an eternity, the bus finally arrived at the station, my ride picked me up and drove me to where I would be staying. I unpacked my things and settled in for my sophomore year of college and year two of playing the role of an adult.

I had made a few small strides in terms of social maturity. My summer job in the city had served a dual purpose. It had been good for me to work and interact with different people, especially those of different ethnicities. It afforded me the opportunity to see that people are generally the same regardless of their skin tone. I learned that we all have the same basic needs, we simply employ different means of satisfying those needs, and in my opinion, that is fundamentally what makes us different. I believe that God created the first couple, Adam and Eve, in His image, and we all descended from them, which indicates to me that we have more in common than some people may wish to admit.

My sophomore year was special. It was official that I had a boyfriend, and we were growing in our relationship, or at least that was my perception at the time. He was someone who did not attempt to take advantage of me sexually. He was a genuinely nice guy, very handsome, and had a wonderful physique. I loved his broad shoulders and always felt a sense of protection and security when he put his arms around me. It felt right, unlike the feeling when other guys had put their arms around me. I was confident that he would not do anything to violate me. I was proud to call him my boyfriend, and even more proud to be seen with such a handsome young man and to know that he loved me, especially since I knew he was the desire of many of the other girls. That cute, shy boy whom I had met in sixth grade, the same one who had grown into such a stand-up guy that was a wonderful support to me when Grandpa died was now my serious boyfriend, we were going steady. When I returned from the city, he had already made his decision to join the military, but not before proposing marriage to me. The poor guy had not outgrown his shyness and had a lot of trouble getting the words of his proposal verbalized. However, he managed to ask me, with some interpreted assistance in clarifying his repeated phrases— "Will you? No, you won't," "Will you? No, you won't." I finally asked him if he were trying to ask me to marry him. He immediately replied, "Yes!"

In my effort not to appear too anxious and to play just a little bit hard to get, I responded, "I'll have to think about it." I was quiet for approximately two or three minutes, before I accepted his proposal and relished in the delight of seeing that proud smile on his face. It was as if he had just been presented with a golden trophy. I don't know which one of us was the proudest, him for being engaged to me or me for being engaged to him.

I believe his proposal was another step in God's plan for putting my life on course. Being married to a serviceman was instrumental in getting me in the appropriate location both spiritually and geographically to actualize my calling and life's work. It absolutely amazes me how God works things for His glory and our story.

Sophomore year in college brought several significant changes. I became engaged to be married and learned that, after nineteen years of being an only child, my parents were expecting a new baby. The news of a little brother or sister was exciting, and I was filled with anticipation of his/her arrival. In addition, my grandmother moved close by. I was able to leave the room that my parents were renting for me and moved in with her. The move worked out well for me. My parents no longer had to pay for my room and board which resulted in more money for the family. They were able to send extra money to me for things that I needed or desired to take part in at the college. As a result of moving out of the boarding home, my parents were able to financially assist my grandmother from time to time, which made life a little easier for her as well.

My stress level declined, I finally settled into college work and my grades improved significantly. Now that I was engaged, I didn't party quite as much. I took the maximum credit load, worked hard, completed a couple of summer sessions, and was finishing my degree requirements a semester early. I didn't know it then, but God was working things out.

My Story

PART VII

I will instruct you and teach you in the way you should go; I will guide you with my eye.
—Psalm 32:8 (NKJV)

My fiancé finished his basic military training and was stationed at his first duty station in the eastern part of the country. Over the next two years, we strengthened our long-distance relationship by talking on the telephone as often as possible. We only got to see each other when he came home on his yearly leave.

We decided to get married over the Christmas break during my senior year in college because I would be completing my degree requirements soon thereafter. He came home on leave, and we went to the courthouse to apply for our marriage license only to be told that I was not old enough and had to have a guardian sign for me. That came as somewhat of a surprise. I was in the process of completing my final semester of college and was going to be twenty-one in a few weeks and still needed a guardian to sign for a marriage license. I had the misconception that I was an adult at this point in my life. After all, I had been basically on my own and making decisions for myself, even though many of them were irrational, since age seventeen.

Rules were rules, there was nothing we could do about it except go back home and ask my grandmother to come with us to the courthouse and sign the consent form for me. She agreed. My grandmother very rarely said no to anything I asked of her. In a few days, we got our license. Norris expedited our blood test results by saying he was being deployed to Vietnam in a few days and wanted to get married before he left. That was not a true statement, but it got him the desired results. We needed to get married quickly because he was due back at his base in thirty days.

We had no money and consequently could not afford to have the formal wedding of my dreams. As a result of being broke, I decided to take the suggestion of a friend, and we got married at my grandmother's home. My friend agreed to be my bridesmaid, and her boyfriend who didn't even know my fiancé served as his groomsman. With only one bridesmaid, one groomsman, the preacher, his wife, my grandmother, and her friend, our marriage took place.

My parents couldn't make the trip to see us get married, but they prepared a nice reception for us in the city. My husband's mother arrived late to the event and missed our entire marriage ceremony. Speaking of late, we were also late due to last-minute details. No bride should have to get married without a bouquet, regardless of budget limitations. The lady at the florist shop gifted me with a beautiful bouquet that she constructed using one white carnation and ribbons. Carnations are my favorite flowers. The bouquet was simple yet beautiful. We picked up our marriage license and rushed back to my grandmother's home for the ceremony. Everyone was waiting when we arrived. I got dressed into my wedding gown. I had made it myself from white satin material, and I made my veil from a piece of cardboard covered with satin and white organza net. I had learned from my mother to take what you have and make what you want. Even though my attire was extremely low-budget, I felt absolutely beautiful.

1965

I remember the look in my groom's eyes as I entered the room. The look in his eyes and the smile on his face made me feel even more beautiful. I was so excited. My heart was pounding, and my hands were shaking from the adrenaline that was pumping uncontrollably. From the look on the face of my soon-to-be husband, I think he must have been feeling the same type of adrenaline rush.

Our feelings of blissfulness were short-lived. Our first disagreement as man and wife was about the trip to the reception that my parents had planned for us. It took place almost immediately after the ceremony ended. My new husband was traveling with very limited funds but had not shared that information with me. He informed me that he would not be attending the reception but did not tell me the reason was because he couldn't afford the trip. If he had been forthcoming with that information, our initial disagreement probably would not have taken place, at any rate not at that time.

After encouragement from my pastor who had just performed our marriage ceremony, and many tears of disappointment from my eyes, the poor guy gave in. He couldn't bear seeing me cry.

He apparently borrowed some cash for the tickets. We went to the bus station, got our tickets, and spent our wedding night riding the bus to the wedding reception that my parents had planned for us. As I look back on that night, I'm sure that was not how he had planned to spend his wedding night. That was just one example of my immaturity. I had no idea of what traditionally took place on wedding nights. My only focus was getting to the party.

The trip was an adventure. There was a problem with my husband's luggage when we arrived at the bus station in Chicago. The reception was planned for the evening of our arrival. My parents had purchased a beautiful outfit for me to wear, but my husband had only the clothes that he had traveled in and no money to purchase an outfit for the event. His luggage was promised to him the next day. The arrangements were in place for the party to happen that evening, and it was too late to postpone it. No one had anticipated misplaced luggage.

Disappointed and embarrassed, Norris refused to come out of the bedroom, nor did he tell anyone that he had no money. He was either too embarrassed or too proud to ask my parents for help, which I am sure they would have gladly given him to help make the celebration special for us.

Our guests arrived, and I celebrated without my groom, which was another indication of my immaturity. What new bride celebrates a wedding reception without her groom? I've learned over the years that for every situation encountered there is a life lesson. What I learned from our wedding fiasco is that it does not matter how poorly the start, what matters most is how successfully we run the race. Our marriage began with much uncertainty and immaturity, but I'm confident that it was the grace of God that kept us together. We did not have much time with each other after getting married. We did not even have a honeymoon. We spent a couple of days at my parents' apartment in Chicago before returning to my grandmother's home and then spent a few days at his parents' home before he had to return to his base. Our time together went by very quickly.

He returned to the military base. I remained to complete my final degree requirements and then returned to live with my parents in Chicago at the end of the semester, rather than joining my husband to begin our lives as husband and wife.

Remaining in the city rather than going to live with my husband was a part of the process that I believe God was using to refine me. There were some areas that I needed instruction in. Going back to Chicago gave me an opportunity to meet a very special co-worker. She was a cheerful young lady. She always wore a bright smile but did not socialize with many of the young people at work. To my amazement, she seemed to gravitate toward me almost immediately. I didn't understand it then, but as I look back using more mature eyes and wisdom, I now see rather clearly that God was using her to impact my life. I think God is very intentional, and this young woman was a part of a greater plan. It wasn't a coincidence that she gravitated in my direction and that our friendship developed so quickly and powerfully.

She would seek me out each day during break time and lunch. We shared stimulating conversation as she shared with me about the love of God. It was impressive to me that she could drive and owned her very own car. The fact that it was in the 60's and much turmoil was taking place in terms of racial issues spilling over from the civil rights movement, coupled with the fact that she was Caucasian and I was African-American, did not seem to matter to her at all. It was as if she did not see color.

That was amazing to me since I had been raised in an environment where color was a great divide. There was something unique about her that I couldn't quite figure out. She seemed to genuinely enjoy my company and required nothing from me in return. I found that to be very thought-provoking, considering I had become accustomed to people befriending me who had hidden agendas.

Most of my associates had been on the take in one form or another. This young woman's only agenda was to share my company and the love of God. She was open and forthcoming about it. I was very comfortable in her presence and before long, I did not see color when I was with her either. We shared a genuine friendship, expecting to gain nothing from each other except the pleasure of companionship.

I didn't understand it then that she was different from my other associates because she had a personal relationship with God. I remember being invited to one of her church meetings. She picked me up in her Volkswagen Beetle, and we drove to the auditorium where the meeting was taking place. There were more people singing, clapping, and who appeared to be having an awesome experience gathered there than any church service I had ever attended. I'd never experienced anything like that before, and I never forgot how genuinely happy the people appeared to be.

When the time came for me to leave the city and join my husband, my friend gifted me with a personal-sized Bible she had autographed with instructions on how to grow closer to God and experience His love.

Her inscription:

Read at least one chapter every day even when you don't feel like it and your life will be enriched by the divine promises contained in His Word.

May the Lord richly bless you as you begin your new life.

Your friend,
Irene

Proverbs 3:5 & 6

Bible from Irene

That Bible was/is special to me. I cherished it and have continued to cherish it until this day. It has become worn and is now falling apart from use, but whenever I look at it, I recall the special friend that I am confident God gave me as a first step in facilitating my healing, and how He used her to begin a growth process in my life for which I will always be grateful. I do not believe that meeting this young woman and sharing her friendship was coincidental. I am certain that it was an important part in my process for which I am thankful.

I worked for nearly a year, celebrated Christmas with Momma, Daddy, and my beautiful little sister, Debra, before joining Norris in New Jersey, December 1966, to begin our lives together as husband and wife.

Front: Debra; Back: Daddy, Me, Momma

Life as a married woman was different and challenging. I had been all about education and earning a paycheck working outside the home. There were so many things that I needed to learn about being a wife and the responsibilities of running a home. I had not learned to cook or keep house. I remember mopping the floor for the first time. Instead of mopping my way out of the room, I mopped my way into the room and had to walk over the wet floor to get out. Norris had learned the proper way to mop a floor during his basic military training. When he corrected my error, I remember feeling very embarrassed and inadequate. Due to my self-esteem issues, I took his efforts to be helpful as a personal affront. My feelings were hurt for days, and I refused to mop another floor for many years after that incident. The mopping of floors became his job.

My reaction was not just another example of my immaturity, but it was also a residual of past abuse. Abuse affects one's ability to interpret the motives of others. Instead of accepting his help as a learning experience and using it as a process of growth, my perception was that I was being judged, and he was pointing out my inadequacies.

I immediately assumed that he was making fun of my lack of knowledge, and somehow that made me feel as though I was not good enough. The feelings that I had experienced in high school resurfaced.

He was very patient with me and did what he could to help me and spare my feelings. I couldn't cook but he ate whatever I prepared and never complained. I remember the first cake I baked for him. It looked very good on the outside, and I felt proud of my accomplishment. When he attempted to cut a slice, to my horror, it was not completely baked even though it looked done from the outside. The cake was not edible, but he attempted to save the day by eating a piece. Unfortunately, my day was already beyond salvaging at that point. I was deeply embarrassed and felt like a failure. I did not know that I could poke it with a toothpick or insert a knife to test for doneness. I had only made banana pudding and ambrosia in Home Economics class in school and therefore had no idea how to bake a cake. Momma had not taught me to cook because Daddy was very particular about his food and would not eat it if he knew I had cooked it. Since we could not afford to waste food, she always did the cooking.

Norris was very attentive. He and I did everything together from cleaning the apartment to doing grocery shopping and the laundry. We used only one pillow because I slept in his arms every night. The two of us even ate from the same plate most of the time. We did not own a washer and dryer; therefore we spent what seemed like hours together at the local laundromat each week waiting for a washer or dryer to become available. We washed our clothes and together folded them, packed them in baskets and made the trip back to our small apartment and put them away. Now that I think about it, perhaps he accompanied me to do laundry so that I would not ruin his uniforms.

I have learned a lot over the years. I can now clean, cook, and do laundry, but most of the things that we did in the beginning have never changed. We continue to do things together, fifty-three years later, however, we do eat from separate plates now and use individual pillows to sleep.

I'd never been left alone for long periods of time and never at night. I remember being terrified alone in the apartment at night, because my husband worked the night shift. I suffered serious adjustment issues as a result.

I remember staying awake most nights. I kept a kitchen knife close by the bed for protection. The idea of having a knife for protection was something I had learned from Daddy. He always carried a switchblade and had given me one when I was a teenager as a means of protecting myself. Thank God I never had to use it. It was frightening being alone at night. I always imagined that someone was going to break into the apartment and hurt me. I feared greatly for my safety. I stayed awake, petrified mostly all night every night. Occasionally I would doze perhaps an hour or so, then suddenly awaken and remain awake until dawn. When my adjustment problem reached a point of severity that I didn't even recognize Norris and almost stabbed him one morning as he arrived home from work, he realized that it was time to take my issues seriously and requested a shift change. His request was granted by his supervisor.

Having him close by had always given me a sense of security. There was something about his presence that made me feel safe. Perhaps it was his strong, no-nonsense, and calm personality that reminded me of the love and security that I had experienced as a young girl being near my Grandpa since Norris appeared to have a similar personality. I don't know. I just knew that with him around I felt safe. From the very beginning of our relationship, I could sense that he was concerned about protecting me and providing that which was in my best interest as much as possible. He treated me as though I was a fragile little object that he cherished and needed to take care of.

My issues with anxiety and depression were not new. I had struggled with anxiety and depressed mood from childhood through high school and college. I had been prescribed tranquilizers following the end of my freshman year of college at eighteen years of age. I think my issues were mainly residuals from my childhood experiences. It wasn't long before I began to develop stress related medical issues such as digestive problems, heart palpitations, circulatory and immune complications. I also struggled with food cravings, especially high carbohydrate foods. My weight yo-yoed up and down. I remember having as many as three sizes of clothing in my closet at any given time.

I made a common mistake that many young brides, especially those with unresolved issues, tend to make. In my ignorance of relationship dynamics, coupled with immaturity, I placed unrealistic expectations on my husband and on our marriage. Like many survivors, I expected him to be the answer to every one of my problems, and I subconsciously expected him to meet each of my needs, even the unspoken ones. Norris had no idea of my unresolved issues and, furthermore, he had his own demons to fight, so to speak. Neither of us had shared with the other in terms of our past individual issues. We just quietly expected everything to resolve itself because we now had each other. I think we each silently expected the other to be a savior. We had the misconception that our love would conquer all our problems. We were both prime candidates for a much-needed reality check.

With our unrealistic expectations, we set in motion a cycle of disappointment and brokenness. I had expected a young man who had never seen a healthy love relationship demonstrated between a man and a woman to automatically know how to have that type of loving relationship with me. I expected him to show me love in the way that I wanted it to be shown even though I had not verbalized to him what I wanted or needed.

I had this idea in my mind of what love looked like, though I had not observed the type of love that I desired in any place other than the movies and television shows. The love that I desired was my own personal fantasy which existed only in my thoughts and dreams, yet I expected those thoughts and dreams to be satisfied by a man who did not have a clue in terms of what was going on in my mind. That's another example of how abuse tends to distort one's perceptions, and my perceptions were surely distorted. When I look back and review the situation with mature vision, so were his perceptions. He had mastered the art of physical caretaking; however, the emotional caretaking that I so desperately craved was virtually nonexistent.

After many years of making and breaking his promises of making me happy, I began to realize that he was struggling with many of the same issues as I. He had his own childhood residuals that had impacted him emotionally. He was fighting with all his might to do the impossible, because his perceptions of what was and was not possible was obviously just as distorted as mine.

Norris was dealing with the aftermath of emotional neglect which is a form of abuse that is just as damaging as any other type. I was seeking emotional support from a man who had never received it, and had not learned how to give it. He shared with me later in our marriage that he had not been told as a child by either of his parents that they loved him. Norris had not experienced the loving compassion that I craved from either one of his parents.

He was an adult with his own family before he heard the words, "I love you" from his mother and said that he could not remember ever hearing those words uttered from his father's lips. As a child, he had never experienced the warmth of a loving embrace from either of his parents. His parents, as so many other poverty-stricken ones, had struggled to keep a roof over his head, food on the table, and clothes on his back as a means of showing their love without realizing that children need to hear loving words and feel gentle strokes for the development of healthy emotions.

As I look back with a renewed perspective, I realize how unfair I had been to him and have come to realize that my happiness has never been contingent upon the actions of another person. Happiness is a choice I make for myself based upon how I interpret what is taking place in my environment at any given time. My happiness was and always has been my own responsibility. I thank God for that revelation. I had been ignorantly and unfairly attempting to make it my husband's responsibility, and he had unwittingly accepted that impossible task. I believe God kept us committed to each other through our tumultuous adjustment period as newlyweds. I continued my fight with stress-related illnesses and was in and out of doctor's offices. My husband did the best he could with his limited skills in terms of being attentive to my needs. The doctors prescribed sleep aids, anti-anxiety medications, and medications for gastrointestinal issues. I took them periodically for approximately five years without much success.

After about three years passed, we finally began to adjust to our lives as husband and wife. I had secured a job with the Board of Education, and we were making progress in our relationship as well as in our finances. We were having more good days than bad when Norris came home from work one day and announced that he was being deployed on an isolated tour to Thailand for an entire year.

He was going to be away from me for twelve whole months. His news hit me in my gut like a brick. I was learning that he was G. I. (government issue) and when the military said, "Go," he had no other choice but to go.

Norris

There was no way of getting out of it unless he had some form of hardship. My issues were real, but not considered hardship by military standards. He was going to be deployed, and there was no way of getting out of it.

That was another major stressor in my life. I think my anxiety began to build as soon as I heard the news. The thought of him leaving me alone was devastating. He knew I would be afraid to live alone and discussed with me the possibility of having someone come and stay with me in the apartment. I would need to resign from my teaching position and return to live with my parents for a year or find someone to stay at our apartment with me because living alone was not an option. We both knew I would not survive that experience for an entire year.

We decided that it would be best for us financially if I kept my teaching position and remained in our apartment. To alleviate some of my fear of being alone, he asked one of his family members to stay with me until he returned home. I would not be alone, but knew things were not going to be the same without Norris. I would not feel the same sense of security with him out of the house. He had become both my rock and security blanket.

I had come to rely on Norris, and he relied on me. We somehow convinced ourselves in the progression of our relationship that we were all each other had and needed. That faulty thinking did not serve me well at all. The Lord was putting me in place to receive some divine instruction.

I remember the night he left. A friend drove us to the airport. I remember the lump in my throat as I watched my husband, my security, the one who had become my strongest supporter, board that plane leaving me alone and unprotected for an entire year. My heart was breaking. It was as if a part of me boarded the plane and the other part was left standing at the airport. I felt torn, afraid, and abandoned. As I stood there frozen in place, I felt the warmth of my tears as they streamed from my eyes, down my cheeks, meeting under my chin and dripping down my neck onto the center of my chest. Our friend waited with me until we saw the plane make its ascent and disappear into the clouds.

On the ride back to our apartment, I was crying so hard that I could barely breathe. Thank God our friend was a man of faith. I remember him stopping the car and encouraging me with words of comfort from the Scripture until I was able to compose myself a bit. He drove us back to the apartment and encouraged me more, assuring me that God would bring my husband and his friend home safely. He made it a point to stop by periodically just to check on me, as he had promised Norris he would do. He was a good friend and has remained a wonderful friend to this day.

I did not handle my stress very well during that year. I started drinking alcohol every night and smoking more and more cigarettes which contributed to my lack of wellness. I remember calling the liquor store for deliveries a couple of times a week for my alcohol of choice. I frequently added a shot or two to a glass of milk because that seemed to give it less burn and allowed the drink to go down smoother. I guess the store manager got to know my voice because one night I called for alcohol and was told that I didn't need it, and my order was never delivered that evening. I remember being furious. How dare him tell me what I don't need! Thinking back, I believe that must have been an act of God. How many liquor store managers will tell a good customer that they don't need an order and refused to deliver? That incident served as somewhat of a wake-up call. I didn't stop drinking, but I was more aware of how much alcohol I consumed after that.

We were blessed that Norris had not been deployed to the area where the real military conflict was happening, but I could not appreciate it as a blessing at that time. I had trouble seeing past my selfish desires of not wanting to be left alone. I was behaving as a spoiled child throwing temper tantrums because I couldn't get my way. His assignment was supposed to have been for one year without vacation. He managed to come home for a few days, six months before his year was up. I still don't know how he pulled that one off. He didn't tell me, and I didn't ask. I was just thrilled to have him home even if he needed to go back.

The year passed slowly, and his tour ended. My husband returned home unharmed with several silk handmade gift items for me. I was filled with excitement to have him home again. Having him with me, however, did not help with my physical complaints. My problems continued to manifest themselves. I later learned that my problem was a spiritual one that was presenting itself in a physical manner.

Our mind, body, and spirit work in unison. Either can disrupt the other when one is out of harmony. As a child I had grown up in church and knew of God but had not learned how to develop a personal relationship with Him. I think my issues were the catalyst to revealing my lack of relationship, and He was drawing me into a love connection with Himself. My life as I had known was on the verge of a major and much needed transformation. I believe that God was continuing to instruct me in the way I should go.

After returning home from Thailand, Norris was assigned to a new base. At the end of the school year, I took a leave of absence from my teaching position. The staff honored me with a going away celebration and gifted me with a beautiful Lenox bowl as a parting gift. I still have that bowl.

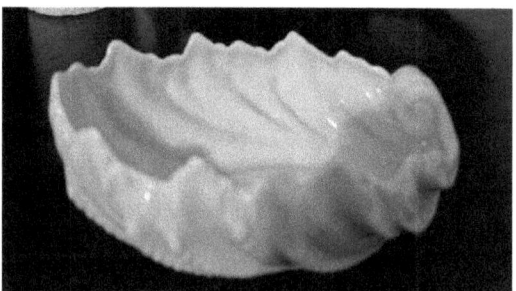

Gift from teachers

The military arranged for the movers to come. They packed-up our things, and we were off to our new home in Plattsburgh, New York. It was a long drive, but we did not mind because we were together. Being together seemed to make even the most uncomfortable situations bearable. We enjoyed the beautiful scenery along the highway as we listened to music with anticipation because neither of us knew exactly what to expect. All we knew about the area was that we were going to be living on the base for our very first time. Living in base housing would be a new experience for us.

Since we began our lives together, we had only lived in off-base apartments. Three of them to be precise. Each had been a little larger and located in a nicer community than the one before. As I reflect on our apartments, I can now see each move that we made as a part of my climb.

We arrived at the next duty station and settled into our new home. The house on base was beautiful. It was much nicer than the apartment in the city we had just left. We had a garage. The first floor of the house consisted of the kitchen, laundry room, and a spacious living room with a patio out front. On the second floor were bedrooms and the bathroom.

Living on the base was considerably different from living in the city. The neighbors were much friendlier, and everyone seemed to look out for the other. It was like the big family that I never had. I felt extremely safe in my environment, and the fear of being alone at night was no longer an issue. I was at last showing some signs of maturity.

We became close with some other couples. The men were in my husband's unit, therefore I had something in common with their wives. Each of them was from a different country. It was fun learning about each other's culture and sharing cultural dishes. It was beautiful to experience how our relationship developed. I thought it was amazing how we came from very different backgrounds yet appeared to have so much in common. Three of us even started our families during the same time, and each of us gave birth to baby girls. How awesome was that? We shared a very special bond before, during, and after the birth of our baby girls.

The thought of becoming a mother was great. Circumstances surrounding my pregnancy made the birth of our daughter even more exciting. Early in my first trimester, I went for my scheduled examination only to be told by my doctor after he had examined me that I was not pregnant. He said that either I had miscarried or had never been pregnant in the first place. He stated that his examination had revealed no signs of life in my womb.

Heartbroken at this news, I drew from the little spiritual training of my past and prayed to God, asking that my baby would somehow still be alive. I guess due to my ignorance of spiritual wisdom I made a bargain with God. I promised to name the baby Hope, if it were still alive. It never occurred to me that if it were alive, it could possibly have been a boy and that name would not have been appropriate.

I was scheduled to have a D and C, dilation and curettage, a few days after that heartbreaking appointment. Upon my arrival for the procedure my doctor examined me again, and to our amazement announced that he had found my baby's heartbeat! I could barely contain my excitement. I was convinced that God had heard and answered my prayers. My pregnancy was an exhilarating time for both of us. It did not matter to me that I suffered morning sickness for the entire nine months, I was enamored with the idea of being pregnant and so was Norris. As our baby grew, he would often rub my stomach and place his ear to it listening for our baby's heartbeat. We were both in love with her before she even entered the world.

Pregnant with Hope

Hope was born a healthy baby following many hours of painful labor. She was born with the help of forceps because I was unable to push her out. Possibly due to the shot the doctor gave me in my spine to ease the pain from my contractions. I was in the hospital on Mother's Day and could not have been presented with a more precious and beautiful gift. Motherhood helped to mature me because I wanted to be the best mother possible. My adorable little girl was our pride and joy, and I worked hard at being the best mother that I could be to her.

I purchased a popular child development book because I wanted to learn as much as I could about how to take care of our baby girl. I referred to it frequently. It was as if that book and I had become the best of friends. If I had a question about introducing a new food, I consulted the book. Whenever I had a developmental question, I consulted the book. Whenever Hope presented with any symptoms, I consulted the book first. My baby girl developed well, and so did my parenting skills.

Baby Hope

Life in Plattsburgh was memorable in that it was different from any place I had lived. It got extremely cold and had more snow than any place that I had ever been before. It wasn't like I had been many places. I'd only lived in three different states—Mississippi, Chicago, and New Jersey. I had seen considerable amounts of snow in Chicago and New Jersey, but the snow in those states did not even compare to the snow we got in the area we were currently living in. I loved the snow and had lots of fun throwing snowballs and making snow people. Even though I was beginning to mature in some areas, I think that I was still very much a child at heart. We both were, it was a lot of fun playing in the snow and throwing snowballs at each other. I remember that there was a significant amount of snow on the ground when we brought our daughter home from the hospital, and she was born in May. My mother and little sister, Debra, came to visit several weeks after our baby was born.

Debra and Momma

Debra was intrigued with butterflies. While playing outside one day, she spotted a beautiful butterfly that captured her attention, and she followed it out of the yard, down the street, and around the corner. She had gone too far and was not able to find her way back home. She was a precocious six-year-old. When she discovered that her surroundings looked different and she was unable to find our yard, she spotted a woman working in her flower garden, approached her, and asked if she would call her sister because she was lost. Debra was not only able to give the woman her sister's name, but her brother-in-law's name as well. The woman looked us up in the base directory and called, informing us of Debra's whereabouts. Momma and I went to get her and found her chatting with the woman while happily enjoying a refreshing snack. I think Momma and I were more upset by the fact that she was lost than she was.

One very memorable evening that later proved to be life-changing for me occurred when Hope was several months old. I received a telephone call from a woman I had worked with at the school. She was much older than I, but I had been supportive to her when she went through her divorce. She and I spent a lot of time together when Norris was away on that isolated tour. She considered me as her best friend. She called me that evening because she had come into the knowledge of salvation through Jesus Christ and wanted to share her life-altering experience with me. As I listened to her conversation, it was apparent that her experience was different from anything that I had ever experienced or heard about, not even in my conversations with the young woman who had given me the Bible several years prior. I was eager to learn more. She shared with me about the change that had occurred in her life since she had developed a relationship with the Lord and described enjoying a type of peace and contentment I longed to have. She called frequently to share with me what she was learning and how her new knowledge and lifestyle was impacting the quality of her life. Her new life sounded very alluring. I was eager to hear more each time she called.

Our assignment at Plattsburgh lasted only eighteen months, and we were re-assigned back to the base that we left in New Jersey. The reassignment was a dual blessing. I was able to get my job back at the school and, in addition, could now see my friend in person for our talks. During our face-to-face discussions, I could see for myself the change in her personality that she had attempted to explain over the telephone. I joined her for church services because I wanted to experience the fellowship she had spoken about. She had been the first one to take me to a nightclub in that area, and now she was taking me to church services. I suppose this is what one might call a 180° turn around. Through her mentorship and fellowship, I accepted Christ as my personal Savior as well, and began to grow in grace and acquire a better understanding of the Word. In addition, I began learning how to apply it to effect change in my life. I began to develop my own personal relationship with the Lord and decided to make some important lifestyle changes as a result. I gave up going to nightclubs, drinking alcohol, and smoking cigarettes. I was approximately twenty-seven-years old at the time but felt much older. I guess because when one lives life as I had been, it tends to age you in some ways. I was very serious about the relationship I was building with the Lord because I was ready for a change. My friend told me I could not build a strong relationship with God and continue to go to nightclubs, drinking, and smoking. I was seeking the joy and peace that she assured me would come from a solid spiritual relationship and decided that those things would not stand in my way.

Before I realized it, my body was responding to the lifestyle changes that I initiated in a very positive way. I no longer had a need for the anti-anxiety medications and was feeling much calmer without it than I had felt while taking it. Several months had passed before I remembered that I had not been taking any anti-anxiety medication.

That realization was exciting. My life was changing. I was experiencing what it meant to have a personal relationship with the Lord as well as what it meant to present my body as a living sacrifice to Him. I sacrificed my old life of drinking, cursing, smoking, and going to night clubs, for a new life in Him. It was a beautiful and rewarding experience in several ways. I am confident that God was continuing a process to make me ready for His use.

My Story
PART VIII

**Behold, I will bring to it help and healing; I will heal them
and reveal to them the abundance of peace and truth.**
—Jeremiah 33:6 (NKJV)

A s I studied the Scriptures, I began to make personal applications to my life. My relationship with the Lord developed and grew stronger and stronger as time went by. I began to see that there is an important difference between knowing of Him and having an intimate relationship with Him. I had known of Him from a child, when I was on that mourner's bench, but never developed a personal relationship with Him. As my relationship strengthened, so did my physical body. My need for peace and security that I had always expected my husband to fulfill began to shift. I learned that it was not healthy to expect my husband to satisfy those needs, and I began to look to the Lord for the fulfillment of my needs instead. My life changed, and my faith was strengthened day-by-day. It was absolutely fascinating how the Lord worked. I showed kindness and support to a woman who was distraught because of her recent divorce, and I was repaid with priceless blessings from the Lord! When we show kindness to others, we never know how that kindness will be returned.

My friend came by frequently, picked me up, and we rode together for services at the church. Norris declined to go. She and I faithfully attended Wednesday night Bible study and prayer meetings, Friday night, Sunday morning, and evening services. We were busy but I was anxious to learn as much as possible about this new way of life that was providing hope, help, and healing for my mind, body, and spirit. I felt that God was changing me from the inside out. It felt great, I was happy, and the change was visible to all who knew me well.

Norris noticed that I had changed. He also noted my commitment to the Lord; however, he misinterpreted my frequent attendance at church as commitment to the pastor. Out of curiosity, and perhaps a slight bit of jealousy, he made the decision to come to a service, not for spiritual reasons, but to see what the pastor was all about. After listening to the Word being preached, my husband was convicted and decided to give his heart to the Lord as well. I was happy and somewhat surprised to see him walk down to the front of the church when the invitation to salvation was extended. Norris made a commitment to live his life from that day forward for Christ. We then began to attend church services together as a family, Norris, our baby girl, and me.

Our lives began to change in positive ways. Not only did my physical health improve, but our financial health began to improve as well. We purchased our first home when I was in my late twenties and Norris was in his early thirties. God showed us favor. The couple selling the home was retiring and moving into a smaller place. They were impressed with us and said that they wanted us to be the new owners of their home so that we could raise our beautiful daughter in the home where they had enjoyed raising their family. I remember that we were short five hundred dollars on the closing cost and needed to postpone the closing date on the home purchase for a few days until we received our next paychecks.

Again, God showed us favor. The seller reached into his pocket, took out his wallet and gave five hundred in cash to Norris so that we would not need to postpone the closing date. He trusted us to return his cash in two weeks as promised, which we did. In addition to loaning us money for our closing cost, the couple wanted to leave their beautiful antique dining room set with the home because it was too large for their new apartment. To ensure that we could afford the exquisite antique, they made us a deal that we could not refuse. Not only did they virtually give us a valuable ten-piece antique dining room set, but they also gave us several beautiful porcelain antiques as well. I didn't realize that porcelain had value until I recently saw one of the pieces on the Antiques Roadshow and discovered its worth. That is just a few of many examples I could give of how God was blessing us and showing us favor.

Our home was beautiful and in an ideal location with a lovely park across the street. The park was convenient. I simply had to walk across the street, and Hope could play on the rides and visit the animals. She loved feeding the ducks. Our home had a lovely sunroom on the front of the house. The living room, formal dining room, eat in kitchen, powder room, and a back porch was on the first floor. There were three bedrooms and a bath on the second floor. We had a third-floor attic area that my husband used as his prayer room. We also had a full basement and a detached garage. We were very happy in our home and thankful to have been favored by God. Home ownership was added to my list of family firsts. We were the first young couple in the family to own a home.

After several years, we decided that we wanted another child. Norris had desired a boy when Hope was born, and we wished our next child would be a boy. We tried several years to get pregnant unsuccessfully.

The doctors said that I had a severe case of endometriosis and would never be able to have another child. I remember how Norris and I prayed, the church and the pastor prayed, as we continued our efforts to get pregnant, even though the medical professionals said that we would never be able to have another child. God said otherwise. We finally got pregnant, and I gave birth to another beautiful baby girl but not before experiencing a little drama.

We were approximately a twenty-five-minute drive from the base hospital where my baby was to be born. I had several false alarms when I thought I was in labor. Norris rushed me to the hospital each time, only to be told that I was experiencing Braxton Hicks contractions and sent back home. When the actual labor pains began, I ignored them thinking they were only Braxton Hicks. After being in labor several hours and the pain intensifying, I contacted the hospital and was told to get there immediately. I am sure the twenty-five-minute drive was done much faster. After arriving at the hospital, we were informed that we needed to go to another military facility because the one where we were was experiencing a problem with the fetal monitoring system and could not safely deliver our baby. They put me in an ambulance, with a police escort. Norris was following behind, and we broke speed limits getting to the next hospital which was approximately a half-hour drive. When we arrived at the hospital, a nurse met me on the sidewalk to escort me to the birthing area. My contractions were coming quickly and strongly. I can remember the nurse saying, "You better not have that baby on the sidewalk." I am sure she was making a joke, but at that point in the process I was not in a mood for humor.

I was immediately prepped for delivery of my baby. The doctor apparently did not have time to read my pre-natal history carefully, because he said I was having a big baby and would have to push, therefore I could not be given an epidural. He told me that I needed to feel the contractions in order to push.

The pain was unbearable. After making an announcement that I could not do it and preparing to die on the table from the excruciating pain, I finally delivered our beautiful baby girl, again with the assistance of forceps, and she was not even seven pounds.

Norris was hoping for a boy, but he could not have been more thrilled when he was presented with another gorgeous baby daughter. He had not been allowed into the delivery room when Hope was born, but by 1976, the rules had changed. He accompanied me into the delivery room to watch as our beautiful new baby girl made her entry into the world. Norris was elated to have another baby daughter; however, he could not bear watching me suffer pain. He prided himself on his ability to protect and comfort me, but during labor and delivery was powerless to do so. When the birthing process was finally over, he said, "No more." Norris never wanted to see me endure that intensity of pain ever again. Having a son was no longer important to him. He decided, at that moment, this would be our last child.

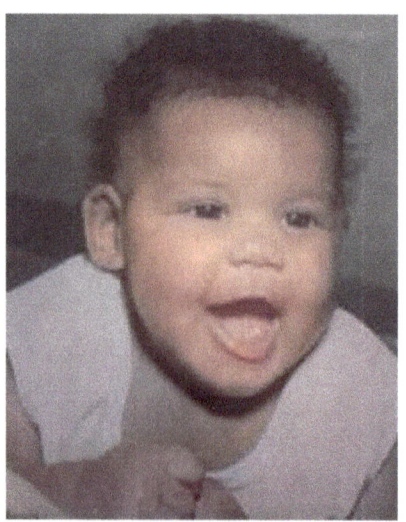

Baby Rae

We called her Rae, which was short for her middle name Rachelle. She was a gorgeous little ball of energy and brought us much joy. Her personality was the opposite of her sister's. Hope was quiet and reserved, whereas, Rae was bubbly and entertaining. She could always be heard singing, clapping or talking. Hope enjoyed retreating to a quiet place with her Barbies or a book. I considered both of my girls to be miracles, since neither of them should have been born according to the doctor's report.

Our family photo

We lived in our home that God had so bountifully blessed us with, happily enjoying our lives, our two precious girls, and our Lord until it was time for our next change of duty station, as Norris called it in military jargon.

Norris was a career airman, and we were in the military for the long haul. This time the assignment was four years in Europe. Even though we loved our home and had enjoyed every moment living there, we didn't want to take a chance on renting it while we were away because we did not know if we would be returning to that area.

We decided to put our home up for sale. To our astonishment, it had nearly tripled in value in less than ten years. Again, I believe God was continuing to show us favor.

The new assignment was bittersweet. I was enjoying my life at the church with my spiritual sisters who had become my friends and confidants. I was going to miss them, my church, as well as working at the school with the children and parents that I serviced. It was, on the other hand, somewhat exciting to have an opportunity to live in Europe. That had been one of the places I dreamed of going to as a young girl when I would sit under that big old tree at the edge of the yard outside of our little shanty. This assignment was going to be a dream come true. Directly after learning we were going to Germany for sure, I purchased language records and attempted to prepare myself for our new home. I thought it would be important if we were prepared to communicate with the German people using their language, even though many of them spoke English, I wanted to be prepared just in case.

God continued to show us favor. Norris had to report to the base and secure housing before the girls and I could join him. We were told it was going to take some time for base housing to become available. He had been informed that he would have a long wait before his family could join him because he would not be able to find an apartment off base. Here again, God showed us favor. It was customary for the military to assign a sponsor to soldiers being transferred abroad. Norris' sponsor was in the process of moving from his off-base apartment into base housing. He arranged with his landlord to secure a contract for his apartment in Norris' name, which provided a seamless transition for us. Rather than having to wait for several months for base housing to became available, it only took two weeks before the girls and I were able to join their father in Germany because an apartment had already been secured for us.

The flight was very long but pleasant. Norris and his sponsor met the girls and me at the airport and drove us back to the apartment. My first ride on the Autobahn was quite a chilling experience. Every car seemed to have been driving at least one-hundred-twenty miles per hour. I think I must have begun to experience some jet lag as soon as the plane landed, which worked in my favor. I remember drifting in and out of consciousness as we zipped in and out of traffic on the Autobahn. Norris' sponsor was German and accustomed to Autobahn driving. He got us safely to the apartment.

It was a very nice apartment that was already partially furnished. Most of our household goods were left in storage stateside. The owner of the building was very nice. He and his family also lived in the building. They owned a restaurant on the first floor. He and his wife had two girls approximately the same age as my girls. The girls spoke English and got along exceptionally well with my girls. The children played nicely together, and the four of them spent a lot of time enjoying each other at our apartment when they were not downstairs in the restaurant being treated to pizza or ice cream by the landlord. He or his wife treated the girls to ice cream and pizza frequently. God had blessed us yet again. Every experience was coming together like a puzzle, each piece fitting neatly in its place.

PART IX

In the year that King Uzziah died, I saw the Lord sitting on a throne, high and lifted up, and the train of His robe filled the temple.
—Isaiah 6:1 (NKJV)

est Germany became a place of growth for me, spiritually, socially, and emotionally. I grew spiritually because being away from my spiritual mentors provided me the opportunity to listen to the Holy Spirit for myself without the influence of their input. In some cases, our love and respect for those whom we see as spiritual leaders will hinder our personal growth in that we tend to rely upon them for directions more than we trust the spiritual insights that God has given each of us. Sometimes it is necessary to separate from those who feed us so that we may learn how to eat on our own. An extremely valuable lesson that I learned while living in Germany away from my spiritual mentors was that God saw me as an individual and dealt with me as the unique creation He had formed. My mentors had been tremendously involved in my Christian growth. They had advised me in terms of many things that were important to them, including make-up, size of jewelry, and length of dresses that I wore. Out of my respect for them and my desire to be pleasing to God, I adhered to their suggestions, even though many of them did not make sense to me nor were they in my heart to do so.

While away, I learned that I did not have to dress or act like anyone else. I could be the original that God created me to be, and that He would deal with me as His created original. There are times when it becomes easy to lose ourselves while trying to be the self that others think we should be. In some instances, we are encouraged to mimic others, and other times we simply assume that is what we should do because of our desire to please. I'm afraid that I was guilty on both accounts. An important lesson for me was to always remember that it is counterproductive to spend valuable time attempting to please people. My efforts should always be focused on pleasing God. Just as the prophet Isaiah was able to see the Lord after King Uzziah was no longer present, sometimes we too must leave people, places, and things that distort our vision before we can see clearly enough to experience the uninhibited movement of God in our own lives. As God directed Abraham to leave his family and go to a land that He would show him (Genesis 12:1 NKJV), it may become necessary for us to do likewise so that we can hear what the Lord is saying to us individually.

While living abroad, I learned that God loved me simply because I am me. It became apparent to me that his love for me was not contingent upon my looks or my association with anyone else. Nor was His love affected by any rituals that I participated in. Attending church meetings and participating in ministry had nothing to do with God's love for me, but rather it had everything to do with my love for Him. My revised perspective helped me grow in grace and walk in a kind of freedom in my love relationship with the Lord that I had not known in the ten years prior. Many times, in our efforts to mentor others, without ever realizing it, we tend to stifle the mentees' growth by exerting too much input, which in my opinion, is a form of control.

It's a great thing when a mentor is not overzealous but is sensitive to the Holy Spirit and able to realize when it is necessary to back off a bit and let God be God in the mentee's life.

Not only did my time abroad serve me well spiritually, it was also a time of emotional growth. It was during this time that I enrolled in a counseling psychology master's degree program. Everything seemed to have fallen into place, piece by piece. God was setting me up to do His work. Everything was working out step-by-step because He had ordered my steps from the very beginning of my existence.

I find it incredible how God works! It did not take long before I became bored with strolling the streets of the village and enjoying the delicious German pastries with my baby girl while her older sister was in school. I had been taught from a very early age to be independent. Having my own money allowed me to do that. I decided to put our baby girl in daycare on the base and find a part-time job. The job search didn't take long. I was offered a part-time position at one of the universities on base. There were a couple of universities that had European divisions. However, I was drawn to the one that offered a counseling psychology program. I believe that the Lord directed me there. He had a plan and that university was compatible with the plan. It was the only one offering a psychology degree. As part of the incentive to work for the university, tuition assistance was provided, and I got to interact with the university professors on a regular basis. I took advantage of the tuition assistance and enrolled in their Master of Arts in Counseling Psychology degree program. Part-time employment for the university worked beautifully. It allowed ample time for family and to complete class assignments. Having the professors available was a plus. Whenever I had questions about an assignment, there was always someone willing to help me resolve my issue. The faculty members were very welcoming and worked to create a family atmosphere. Everyone was on first-name basis in the office.

I didn't understand at the time how God was going to use my counseling training. I thought I was drawn to the counseling program to get the needed skills required for assisting the children I worked with in the inner-city school where I had hoped to return after our Germany assignment ended. However, the Lord used my counseling psychology degree program to provide much-needed insight into my inner self. It was like peeling the layers from an onion. Each of the classes provided much-needed awareness for me personally as I began to explore my own personality. They were helpful in providing enlightenment with respect to the negative impact the abuse I had suffered in the past had left on my psyche.

During those times of experiencing the emotional and sexual mishandling that I mentioned earlier, I was not even aware that those events were abuse, and I certainly didn't realize I had trauma residuals resulting from those experiences, nor did I realize that they were affecting the decisions I made or the quality of my life.

As I delved into each of those counseling psychology assignments, I was able to see the toll that my past experiences had taken on my personality more vividly and understand how it had been shaped by each of those past trauma experiences. I realized the psychological damage that had been done due to my experiences, and I learned what steps I could take toward my own healing.

I think my most difficult and important task was to view myself as worthy of respect and love. It is not uncommon for someone who has been treated disrespectfully for a long period of time to begin viewing themselves as unworthy. I believe it is a form of conditioning and response because, in some cases, those who have been habitually disrespected often treat themselves with disrespect. Sometimes, the disrespect is revealed through the absence of self-care, such as a proper diet, exercise, and rest.

That theory proved true in my case—I did not do a good job in terms of self-care at all. My diet was terrible, usually consisting of high-fat and sugary foods. I didn't exercise, and I very rarely got eight hours of sleep.

Here again, I believe that the Lord was preparing me for a ministry of healing the hurt and showing me firsthand that it is possible to suffer residual effects of past traumatic experiences without even realizing what is happening. Many people today suffer from past trauma that affects the way they view the world and interact with those around them, but they don't have a clue as to why they behave and respond to others in ways that are not productive.

I think the Lord was using those counseling psychology classes for my personal growth and development, as well as my spiritual growth and development. As I grew stronger emotionally, I noticed a difference in my perception of how I interpreted conversations and the actions of other people. I began to develop trust, no longer looking for hidden motives in every interaction with others.

In addition to the change, I developed a deeper understanding and a stronger love relationship with the Lord. It became apparent that I needed to be whole first before I could have the empathy required to assist anyone else in their process. It was as if the Lord needed to remove me from what I thought I wanted and placed me in the position to receive what my heart and soul so desperately needed and had been searching for.

I originally thought I needed my spiritual mentors to develop the level of faith they seemed to possess, but I learned that it was not them that I needed.

Rather, what I truly needed was to avail myself more to the spirit of God and allow Him to complete the work that He had begun in my life. The level of faith that my mentors possessed was a gift to them. My level of faith was going to be a personal gift to me. It would be specific to my needs.

Those four years abroad were exactly what I needed to gain the required emotional intelligence to face my unresolved issues honestly and bravely, in addition to vital preparation for my life's mission of healing the hurt of individuals suffering from residuals of emotional trauma, just as I had been.

As I continued growing in grace and delighting myself in Him, I felt like He was giving me the desires of my heart just as the Scripture promised. When I was a little girl sitting under that big old oak tree at the corner of our yard and dreaming, one of the things I frequently dreamed about was that one day I would go to Paris. That dream materialized while living in West Germany. I not only had the opportunity to visit Paris, but also got a chance to spend time in Rome, Switzerland, Holland, Berlin, Luxembourg, Belgium, and a few other places I had read about in books.

Going to Paris, visiting the Eiffel Tower, the Louvre, and seeing the Mona Lisa was a dream come true. I wanted to see those sights for a very long time.

It was also exciting to visit Rome and make the real-world connections with many of the events I had studied in the Bible. Visiting the catacombs and learning how difficult life had been for Christians at that time was sobering in terms of how much we take for granted. That revelation made me extremely grateful for the advances that have been made in terms of religious freedoms. As we toured the ruins of the Colosseum, my mind drifted back to stories read and movies seen.

I soaked up the information presented by our tour guide like a gigantic sponge.

Going skiing in the Swiss Alps was something I had not dreamed about, but it was an awesome experience. I never graduated from the bunny slopes; however, that ski trip will surely be remembered. The girls had a marvelous time playing in the snow, ice skating, and drinking hot chocolate. Hope put on a pair of skis and took to the bunny slopes along with me. We all had an awesome time.

The trip to Holland was very special because Momma had come for a visit, and she was able to enjoy the beauty of the tulip gardens and shops along with us. We purchased wooden shoes for the girls as souvenirs. We made some very special memories, and I will hold them all in my heart and mind forever.

Berlin was an emotional yet educational tour. Seeing the wall and listening to stories about the experiences of the people, especially children being separated from their parents by the wall and not being able to reconnect, was very emotional.

The stories broke my heart, and I remember thinking how grateful I was to have not lived through some of the experiences that our tour guide told us about. I could not imagine the agony of being separated from my darling little girls never to see them again. My life as a child had been difficult but I didn't feel that my difficulties compared to some of the experiences we learned about on that Berlin trip.

Having the opportunity to travel had been one of my childhood dreams, and the Lord was giving me that opportunity. He was allowing me to see each of the cities that were on my dream list, plus some additional ones.

My Story
PART X

Delight yourself also in the Lord, And He shall give you the desires of your heart.
— Psalm 37:4 (NKJV)

Another one of my heart's desires had continuously been to help my mother and bring some happiness to her life. I saw that manifesting. I felt like I was being successful in bringing some joy to Momma's life, because each place that I lived, she in turn had an opportunity to visit and experience the excitement of seeing another part of the world along with me. She had already enjoyed her experience in Plattsburgh, New York, Canada, and New Jersey. Now she was having a good time experiencing Europe and would later have an opportunity to experience Pennsylvania and Texas.

Momma had a childlike way about her. Her excitement showed in her eyes as well as in her body language. I felt a sense of accomplishment as I watched her reaction to visiting places she never dreamed would have been possible for her to ever see. She always posed for an endless number of photos which she used to remember each event and to share with family, friends, neighbors, and anyone else who she could convince to take a look.

We met some wonderful people and established some long-term relationships during our stay at Sembach, Germany, just as we had done at the Air Force Base in Plattsburgh. The girls grew quickly developed relationships with a few girls their ages, and they adjusted well to their environment. That four-year assignment passed very rapidly. We loved living in Germany so much that we decided Norris should extend his stay for an additional four years. He requested and was granted the extension to his assignment. We were excited about the idea of eight years in Europe. I was especially happy about the cultural benefits my girls were acquiring. Life was good, and we were ecstatically happy.

Since we were going to be away for an additional four years, we thought it would be a good idea to come home for a visit. Norris arranged the trip, and we flew home on a military plane. The plane was unlike any I had ever flown on before. It was massive and loud. Take-off and landing were the worst. I am super sensitive to altitude changes, usually experiencing ear pain with the slightest amount of pressure change in the cabin. The airline attendants issued us military grade earplugs that helped tremendously. Overall it was a good flight that did not cost us much money at all. That was the best part of the flight because we were on a tight budget.

I remember the plane needed to stop for fuel in the Azores. That was exciting because it gave us an opportunity to see Portugal, another section of the world that we probably would not have seen otherwise. Even though we didn't have the opportunity to do any touring of the countryside, it was yet very exciting to have landed in the Azores and be able to de-plane, feeling the ground under our feet in Portugal.

We arrived back in the US and made our connecting flights to visit our parents in Mississippi and Chicago. We spent the first half of our time in Mississippi with Norris' parents and the last half was spent in Chicago with my parents.

When it was time to leave for our return trip to Germany, Daddy came into the room to say goodbye to us before he left for work. There was something different about this goodbye. Normally when we visited and got ready to leave, Momma would always have tears in her eyes, but this time Daddy was the first one with tears. I had never seen him get emotional at goodbyes. As he hugged me goodbye, he tearfully said, "Why do you all have to go back over there? I won't see you again."

No one had any idea that he was ill. I had noticed a change in his demeanor during our visit but attributed it to the fact that he had given his heart to the Lord and was now living his life differently. The change was obvious. He no longer used his sharp tongue. He was cheerful and no longer abused alcohol. I didn't feel the need to walk on egg shells around him. He was different, and that felt good. We later discovered that there was another reason for his temperament change. In addition to his relationship with God, Daddy had cancer, and no one knew. Since I had no idea as to why he made the statement or why his disposition was so sullen, I attempted to make a joke in an effort to lighten the mood. I thought if I could get him laughing, that would make him feel a little better about us going back to Germany. I remember saying to him laughingly, "Where are you going? You're not going anyplace," indicating that we would return, and he would indeed see us again. His response was, "I don't know, sometimes I feel pretty bad." He then wiped his eyes and walked out of the room and went to work. Little did I know that would be the last face-to-face conversation Daddy and I would have because he was correct in saying he would not see me again.

We took our flight back to Germany and, within weeks, I received a phone call stating Daddy was sick. I did not know the extent of his illness until nearly three months later. He had lung cancer that metastasized to his brain. He had been able to keep his illness a secret from the family because he was getting his treatment at the veteran's hospital where he was employed. By getting treatments at work, he had been successful in keeping his condition undisclosed. It was only after the cancer metastasized to his brain and his memory was affected to the extent that he began to forget his thoughts, so much so that he was unable to complete his sentences, that Momma became concerned and thought something may be wrong. As a result of his deteriorating memory, he stopped communicating. This was either his effort to cover the fact that he couldn't remember, or he couldn't remember long enough to complete his thought. Daddy was one who always had a lot to say. For him to keep quiet was highly unusual. His refusal to communicate was an indicator that something was seriously wrong. Momma insisted on going with him to the hospital for an examination to find out what the problem was.

She was shocked to discover he had lung cancer and that it had metastasized to his brain. Momma was devastated to learn Daddy did not have much time to live. They had been together since they were teenagers. Even though they had some co-dependent and volatile years, it was obvious they cared deeply for each other. That news was a blow to all of us, and we were praying for him to recover.

I had asked my church family to pray with me for him. We had been taught that anything we asked the Father in the name of Jesus, if we had faith, we could have. We had always been taught in our church to name it and claim it. I asked the Father in the name of Jesus, I named and I claimed healing for my daddy.

He was in the hospital when we got the news of the severity of his condition. When he was discharged, I felt relieved thinking that my prayers had been answered only to hear a short time later that Daddy was dead. I was in a state of shock, confused, and conflicted. I didn't understand how he could be dead after I had prayed in faith, believing my prayers would be answered. I had done everything the church leaders had taught me to do. I had even fasted for my prayer to be answered and yet it was not answered. Daddy was dead. Approximately three months after we had left from our Chicago visit and hearing Daddy say that he would not see me again, Momma conveyed the news to me that he was ill. Then within weeks, she informed us that he had transitioned. Once again, we were making our arrangements to fly from Germany to the United States. This time not for an enjoyable visit, but for Daddy's funeral.

PART XI

Be diligent to present yourself approved to God, a worker who·does not need to be ashamed, rightly dividing the word of truth.
—2 Timothy 2:15 (NKJV)

I remember being very conflicted in my mind and awfully confused. I don't remember ever feeling that level of confusion at any time before. It had been my faith in God that had grounded and brought me comfort up to this point, and now it was my faith that appeared to have been the major source of my pain and confusion. The operative word here is appeared. I learned from my experience that things are usually not as they appear to be. This time of inner conflict and confusion was the beginning of a deeper and more meaningful educational experience for me in terms of my relationship with God and His Word. He had separated me from my former spiritual support persons to deal with me personally. Yet I was holding onto that which He desired to separate me from—my old ways of reacting and thinking. Rather than diligently seeking God for understanding and the strength to accept what he had allowed, I took the path of least resistance, one that required no work on my part. Rather than do what second Timothy 2:15 instructs, I chose to expect a miracle, one that would work in my favor and bring me satisfaction without putting forth the effort required to study Scripture for correct understand.

My prayer was to heal my father. I didn't even bother to consider God's will for my father or my father's will, for that matter. It was all about me and what I wanted to happen, which contradicts Scripture as I have now come to understand it. I had not been diligent in studying Scripture, nor was I rightly dividing *(seeking clarity in terms of interpretation)* His word. What I had been taught in terms of faith, asking and receiving, was all true. However, there was a very important piece in that process that I had failed to take into consideration. Whatever I ask in faith must be according to His will. Then and only then will it be done. My prayer was purely about me and God was not about to reward my selfishness. The essence of *my* prayer had been let my will be done rather than let *Thy will be done.*

Norris was granted an emergency leave from his duty assignment, and we made the trip back to Chicago. The trip to the funeral home is somewhat of a blur. I can remember though that it was a very frigid day in February. Winters in Chicago can get very cold. I can remember being in the room looking at Daddy in the casket. I can't remember if the family was there with me or if I was alone in the room. I do remember, however, feeling overcome by a mixture of emotions. My faulty thinking in terms of Scripture was manifesting as unrealistic expectations that I now believe were bordering on insanity. Here again was an opportunity for me to become one of the unfortunate statistics that make up the population in mental institutions. I think being in such a fragile emotional state, I could very easily have experienced a permanent break from reality, but I believe that God said, not so! Insanity was not part of His plan for my life, and for that I am extremely grateful.

It is astonishing how grief can affect one's ability to think rationally. As I look back and analyze my behavior and feelings with a more spiritually-mature perception, I can now see very clearly that my feelings were motivated by pure selfishness and ignorance in terms of Scriptural interpretation. I had been reading but had failed to study God's Word for understanding.

I had somehow managed in my mental distortion to make Daddy's death all about me. I had unfinished business to discuss with him. It had taken many years for me to build up the courage to confront him with feelings I had held inside since childhood, and now that I had finally developed enough courage to confront those issues with him, he had the audacity to die, denying me my opportunity to confront him. I was angry and felt cheated that he had denied me what I felt was my chance to speak my piece and clear the air between us.

My faulty thinking in terms of Scripture, coupled with a pattern of distorted thinking from past trauma, were resulting in a level of selfishness that had complicated my grief process. I can remember standing in front of the casket that day in the funeral home, looking down on Daddy, and praying silently for him to open his eyes and get up. I can also remember the overwhelming disappointment, sadness, and sense of feeling abandoned by God that I felt when he didn't open his eyes. I felt hopeless and confused. I did not understand why God did not grant my request. Complicated grief coupled with faulty biblical understanding can wreak havoc on one's psyche.

I grappled for several weeks with confusion in terms of God's love for me. Thankfully, I managed to put my thoughts and feelings into perspective before any lasting damage was done to my ability to think rationally or my love relationship with Him destroyed. After I gained enough emotional composure to confront my true feelings and acknowledged them as total selfishness and a lack of Scriptural understanding, I was able to accept what God had allowed and grieve the loss of my father in a healthier manner. Confronting myself and unveiling the ugly reality that I was selfish wasn't easy, but it was a necessary process for my emotional healing to occur as well as a sustained healthy relationship with God.

It was not pleasant having to acknowledge that I prayed daily saying, *Thy will to be done* yet I wanted my will to be done more. I learned I needed to remove myself from the equation and be sincere each time I pray *Thy will be done.*

The girls and I did not return to our home in Germany after Daddy's death. Norris went back to take care of what was needed for another change in his duty station. The girls and I stayed in Chicago to be close to Momma for a while before returning to New Jersey. I was offered a teaching position at the school where I taught prior to moving to Germany. The principal had made me a promise that if I were ever in the area and needed work, there would always be a place for me in his school. God was showing me favor once again. My girls and I moved in temporarily with my brother-in-law and his family. Their daughter was a few months younger than Rae. The girls played together and got along well most of the time. Both girls had tempers, and they clashed from time-to-time, but never anything serious occurred between them. I kept an eye on Rae, and my sister-in-law kept a watchful eye on my niece.

I enrolled both my girls in the private school that my oldest daughter, Hope, had attended previously, and I went back to work for the remainder of the school year teaching an extremely challenging group of third graders. I learned later, after accepting the position that their regular teacher had quit, and the students had been responsible for three previous long-term substitutes leaving the class because of their out-of-control behavior. Those students were challenging but I was up for the challenge, and we endured together as a class until the end of the school year. My degree in counseling psychology paid off well.

Norris was successful in getting his change of duty station. He was assigned to a base in Minot, North Dakota. The movers came and packed up our household items and shipped them to the next duty station. However, in the interim, his assignment was changed to Dyess Air Force Base in Abilene, Texas. We went to Texas, and our household items went to North Dakota. What could have been a large problem for our family turned out to be only a minor inconvenience. We made the best of a bad situation by camping out in the house for several days until our furniture came. There was a place on the base where soldiers could borrow essential items. That was a blessing and enabled us to get through those days of roughing it until our household items arrived. We were fortunate that it was during the summer and the children were out of school. They enjoyed the adventure of camping inside. That was as close as I would ever come to a camping expedition because I could never imagine myself sleeping outside with the critters.

Our time in Abilene was short yet memorable. We met some very nice people who invited us to their church. There seemed to be something special about military families. They often went out of their way to be helpful and make the transition smooth for new arrivals. The church was very welcoming, with a warm and friendly congregation. We joined and became active in the ministry. Once the children were back in school, I found a job and worked at a department store for a couple of months before finding a teaching position at a Christian school. Working at the Christian school was very different from working at the inner-city public school I was accustomed to. I'm not sure if the major difference in the students' attitude toward learning was the fact that it was a Christian environment or northern versus southern values. Whatever made the difference, working at the Christian school in Texas was like a retreat when compared to that third-grade class that I had just left in New Jersey.

I worked in the junior high learning center and from time to time in the high school learning center as well. The students never challenged my authority and always responded in a respectful way whenever there was a need to correct a behavior, which did not occur very often.

Texas weather was extremely hot during the summer. There was a cottonwood tree in our front yard and for some reason it was covered with fuzzy little worms. The worms would somehow fall off the tree and could be seen crawling all over the porch and up the side of the house even getting into the house if the door was left open long enough. I had a fear of worms from childhood and had not overcome that fear. I was always anxious whenever I had to go outside. In addition to the cotton worms, the area was noted for thunderstorms and tornadoes. I was not accustomed to tornadoes and was frightened by them as well. I remember one afternoon as we were sitting around the table having dinner, the news of a tornado flashed across the television urging everyone in the area to take shelter immediately. We had not been briefed in terms of taking shelter during a tornado, nor were we knowledgeable of storm shelters in the area. We just looked at each other and remained seated, not knowing exactly what action we should take. My heart was pounding as if it would jump right out of my chest. It was by the grace of God that I did not experience cardiac arrest or that the tornado did not touch down in our immediate area and blow us all away. It did, however, strike the nearby shopping mall which sustained a significant amount of damage. The worm situation had been frightening enough, but the tornado was more than enough for me to decide that Abilene, Texas was not a place where I desired to live for very long.

I began to put out feelers for employment back on the East Coast shortly after the tornado incident. The sooner I could escape Abilene, the better.

After several inquiries to school districts near Trenton, I received a call to interview for a teaching position in one of the Township school districts. I flew back for the interview, and my old principal apparently saw me someplace in the area. He asked a friend, who was still working at his school, if I were back in town because he had a vacancy and wanted to know if I were available to take it. Some may call that a coincidence, but I call it providence. The position at the Township school did not work out because I believe that God had another plan. I think He was strategically orchestrating every aspect of my life. My friend got in touch with me and gave me the principal's contact information. I reached out to him. He explained the position and assured me that if I wanted it, it was mine. I told him that I was looking for a position in the area and would be happy to return to his school. He was excited to hear that and mailed my contract to me so he would have my signature in time for the upcoming board meeting. I called that God's favor! I don't think teaching contracts are routinely mailed to applicants.

Norris and I discussed it and decided I would go back to New Jersey with the girls, and that he would request a duty change as soon as possible. Norris was near retirement at that point in his career, and I assume that if he had not been granted the base of his choice in New Jersey, he could have retired at any time to join his family.

Again, my brother-in-law and sister-in-law opened their home temporarily for us until we could find a place of our own. Perhaps they were willing to help us out because they had lived with us for a time when they were first married. That was how we did things back then. Families were taught to help each other and share what we had. The love of God and family was not simply verbalized, but it was demonstrated through our actions as well.

Since God was in control and working out the situation for His glory, it didn't take long at all for Norris to get reassigned to McGuire Air Force Base, and we were shopping for a house. We looked at several homes that were close to my work, but the one that we decided upon as the best place to raise our girls was approximately thirty miles away from the city. The home had four bedrooms, two-and-a-half baths, a formal dining room, family room, formal living room, eat-in kitchen, laundry room, and a two-car garage. In addition, it had a large front yard and a backyard space that was ideal for the children to play and for Norris to plant a small garden. He loved working outside and attempting to grow his own vegetables. The home also had a patio out back and mature fruit trees in the front and back yards. I remember Norris and I teasing each other because we mistakenly called the apple tree a dogwood. We had both grown up in the country and picked many apples from trees as children, yet neither of us recognized the apple tree in bloom. It was as if there was a lesson for me in every experience, regardless of the simplicity of the situation. The lesson that I gleaned from the apple tree experience is that our full potential isn't accurately recognizable until fruit is produced in our life.

When the realtor showed us the home, we fell in love with it and knew right away that this was the ideal place. We wanted to raise our girls there. We enjoyed that home for many years. It was not only home for our girls and, later, home for our grandchildren to enjoy, but it served as a welcoming sanctuary for our daughters from other mothers who I lovingly refer to as my *DFAM'S*. God had blessed us, and we made a commitment to use what He blessed us with to be a blessing to others. We shared our home, our time, and resources because we desired to bless others as we believed God was blessing us.

The thirty-minute drive to work daily, sometimes in bumper-to-bumper traffic, became my quiet time. I used it to reflect and meditate. Doing so made the drive more of a relaxing experience than an inconvenience. I considered my position as an elementary school teacher a blessing. It was very rewarding to me personally because I felt like I was making an important difference in the lives of the students and their parents as well. My degree in counseling psychology that I had earned while living in Germany was a great benefit to my success. The paybacks derived from being able to assess my students individual needs from a psychological perspective were a definite plus for working with inner-city youth. I think my counseling background permitted me to build a unique rapport with my students. I was able to look past their unacceptable behavior and see the pain behind the performance. Not only was I able to recognize their pain but had a good idea in terms of how to service them for achieving the desired conduct. Proof that my influence impacted my students in a positive way is apparent because some of them have maintained contact with me even to this day.

I was offered a position to serve as Counselor of Employability Skills for the Youth Corps. I accepted the challenge to work with high school dropouts between the ages of sixteen and twenty-five. My task was to prepare them for job readiness and encourage them to complete their GED. The work was often difficult but extremely rewarding. The position with the Youth Corps sparked my interest in elementary school counseling. I thought if I could use my expertise with younger children, the impact would be greater than attempting to change behaviors after they were well developed as with the high school dropouts. My background was both clinical and educational which was a unique skill set for a school counselor. The Youth Corps was a pilot program. When it ended, I applied and was hired as a professional school counselor assigned to the elementary school. If I were to rate job satisfaction on a scale of 1 to 10, my rating would have been about a 12. I loved my job. It was an awesome experience servicing my students and watching the change in their attitudes and behaviors. Not only did I have a chance to effect change in my students, many of their parents sought my assistance as well. I believed that God was continuing to work His plan through and for me, and I referred to my duties not as work but as my ministry.

Church was always a very important part of our lives. We reunited with our old church upon returning to the area. My spiritual mentor was still there, but I did not need her mentorship as before. Our roles appeared to have shifted, and she came to me often for clarification on issues that she needed to sort out.

When we moved into our new home, we decided to join a church close by. Each of the churches that we had associated with impacted our lives in unique ways but neither of them was where I was destined to find my purpose. Norris and I were serving in ministry at our church, but I never felt as though I was fulfilling my purpose. It was as if something was missing.

One day, a friend invited us to a Bible study at another church she had visited. It was approximately a twenty-minute drive, but we accepted the invitation. One visit was all we needed to realize that there was something extra special in the way this pastor taught the Word of God. Both Norris and I desired more and more. We learned the essence of rightly divining the Word of God. We also learned that there was a vast difference between reading the Word and studying it. We both learned the art of studying the Word. As I studied my Bible and listened to the pastor's teaching, my love relationship with the Lord grew stronger and stronger, and I gained more insight into how the Scripture can be applied to every aspect of life.

One morning after service, our pastor made an announcement regarding a new ministry that was going to be starting soon. Apparently, there had been some discussion about this new ministry because they had already chosen a name for it, and it was to be designed to offer hope, help, and healing for those who were victims of rape, incest, and domestic abuse. He further announced that if anyone was interested in serving on this highly-confidential ministry, they were to contact him personally.

As soon as I heard the announcement, it felt like something resonated in my spirit, and I knew immediately that I wanted to serve on that ministry. I knew personally the devastating pain that abuse could cause and wanted to be a part of helping others suffering, as I once had suffered, to become free. I made the call to express my interest in serving on the ministry. The pastor asked about my background. I did not share any of my personal experiences which I was sure had molded me into being a candidate to serve on such a ministry. I only shared my academic background, and his response was, "Now I know why it has taken so long to get this ministry going, God was waiting for Mary Patton." I initially made that call to speak with the pastor regarding my desire for serving on the ministry. However, he placed me as lead person in charge of the ministry. There was a group of highly qualified individuals that were assigned to work with me. However, I was in charge.

This was what the struggle with my ladder of broken rungs had been all about. I believe God had allowed it all to happen to prepare me for a time such as this. I was embarking upon my life's calling. The brokenness, fear, pain, sexual mishandling, and disappointments that had been my past experiences were all designed to prepare me for this assignment. I had been molded like the clay on a potter's wheel, and now I was a completed vessel ready to be used, or at least that was what I thought at the time. The very thought that

God was going to use me to do this vital work for His kingdom was humbling.

This was my first attempt at designing a ministry. It was my very first attempt at being in charge, let alone structuring a ministry curriculum. I had always been the one who served on but never over a ministry. I was very comfortable working as a support person, always in the background, and never bringing much attention to myself. This task was a bit intimidating yet, at the same time, exhilarating. I was confident this was the direction the Lord was taking me in, and I was humbled to have an opportunity to serve His people for His glory.

My desire, even as a young child, had always been to help others. I had been previously afforded the opportunity to help people in many ways, but this was special. I had experienced up close and personal the havoc that abuse can cause in one's life. I had learned from experience that brokenness resulting from emotional mishandling has the potential to cause severe damage to an individual's relationships, including their relationship with God. Emotional healing is necessary for developing and maintaining a healthy spiritual life. My task was to create a curriculum of instruction that would help ministry participants understand the crippling residuals of abuse, how those residuals could potentially impact their lives, and to further put in place a recovery plan that worked.

My task was not an easy one. As I prayed and sought the Lord for direction, He began to unfold His plan to me step-by-step.

PART XII

Be anxious for nothing, but in everything by prayer and supplication, with Thanksgiving, let your requests be made known to God.
— Philippians 4:19 (NKJV)

here was a sense of accomplishment that came with knowing I was functioning in my gift. I was astounded at the feeling of peace and satisfaction derived from working with the healing ministry. Watching the participants grow spiritually and emotionally was exciting as well as humbling. Exciting because I could literally observe the group participants' spiritual and emotional growth and humbling because I could personally relate to their inner conflict. God was using me as a vessel to accomplish His work of healing in their lives. Upon completion of the twelve-week cycle, some chose to repeat the course, some were competent and demonstrated success by following the call that they felt God had placed on their lives. Some of the group participants became ministers, others became pastors, and some went on to pursue their dreams as entrepreneurs. Group participants over the years ranged from young adults to senior citizens. The devastating residuals of abuse has no age restrictions.

Prayer was always an integral part of the ministry. Each session began and ended with a prayer. I desired for the emotional yokes of abuse to be broken and believed that only God's power could accomplish such a crucial task. The ministry was a very confidential one, and each participant learned the importance of being their sister's keeper. We prayed together, studied together, and celebrated together each time God motivated significant change in someone's life.

Even though I felt that God had elevated me, and I was director and teacher of the ministry, I had not yet fully arrived emotionally. I was continuing to evolve. I was not yet that completed vessel I had assumed to be. The lessons He inspired me to write always appeared to have been for my deliverance as well as for the group. It was as if God used me as the test dummy to prove that the lessons really worked prior to presenting them in the ministry. He knew I yet had some insecurity issues and they often presented as second-guessing myself. God was teaching me that I could trust him to keep His promise. He was reassuring me that He was not like the many others in my life who had made promises they didn't keep. He was letting me know with each new lesson that there was no need for me to hold onto that very familiar anxiety that was always present when I was presented with a challenge. Rather, He showed me that I could be secure in Him, knowing that He was going to meet each need as it was presented to Him. I simply needed to keep my relationship in good standing with Him, and He would use me continuously for His glory and my story.

Letting go of past hurtful experiences was one of my challenges. Some things are easy to let go of, but the closer one is to a person or situation, the more pain can be inflicted, and it becomes difficult to let go of those feelings. I also had problems letting go of residual anxiety that resulted from those past experiences. Certain behaviors or actions would often awaken memories making past experiences like a parrot repetitively chatting phrases in my mind. The memories would just keep repeating themselves. People and things that we are casually connected to are usually not very difficult to release. Letting go of casual things does not pose a significant challenge at all. I have learned from those hurtful times when I had been disappointed because I expected certain people to be in my cheering section only to find that they weren't rooting for me at all, that sometimes unrealistic or failed expectations can cloud one's vision making it difficult to differentiate between letting go of a situation and letting go of the individual. My personal struggle was that in my mind I was afraid that if I let go, I would stop loving the person altogether. I couldn't separate my loved ones from their behavior and what I concluded were offenses toward me. God had to teach me yet another lesson, this time I needed one on forgiveness. I had to accept the fact that letting go involved the process of forgiveness. One will not effectively work without the other being present.

I found myself holding onto the hurt that I believed had been inflicted upon me because, in my mind, I had not done anything to warrant the type of pain I carried from childhood. I held onto a victim mentality. When someone would hit my trigger, seemingly out of nowhere, memories resurfaced and I would feel victimized, taken advantage of, and powerless to change the situation, just as I had felt as a child. I had to acknowledge and process my feelings before I could even think about forgiveness. As I processed my feelings, it became apparent to me that not only was I hurt, but I was also extremely angry which fueled my desire to fight back anytime I became offended. I had wrestled with anger issues from childhood. My temper had also proven to be another one of my most difficult challenges to overcome. I fought back fiercely whenever I became offended because my inner-child was struggling for her position of power. As an abuse survivor, I knew too well that overwhelming feelings of helplessness which often resurfaced when I sensed I was in some way being taken advantage of and not getting something that I felt was deserved. I had developed enough self-control that physical fighting was no longer an issue for me, but I was still fighting whenever I thought there was a need. I mastered the art of using my words very skillfully to cut to one's core. I learned how to fight back viciously while maintaining my lady-like facade. I was teaching my group participants that the Bible has an answer for every situation one may experience. I sincerely believed those words were true, and honestly trusted that if I searched long and diligently enough, I would find my answer in the Scripture as well. My inner fight was hard and real. I knew deep down inside that my feelings were not coming from a healthy place but could not seem to let go of them. I needed His help to forgive those whom I held responsible for my past hurts. I could not do it on my own. He was using me even in my conflicted and anxious state. However, I believed that I could be even more effective if I were able to release the toxic emotions that were buried deep inside of me. Forgiveness was key.

I continued to pray, and my answer eventually came as I began to analyze the question: *What does forgiveness mean to me?* After a considerable amount of contemplation, my response to that question was: *I believe that forgiveness happens when we take away the value of an experience.*

Without value the experience is devoid of power to control our thoughts and emotions. When said experience is no longer important enough to arouse a negative emotion, that's forgiveness. Now that I had my definition, and it made perfect sense to me, the question then became: *How would I make those statements work for me?*

As I pondered that question, I was reminded of a technique I learned in one of my counseling psychology classes used to stop negative thoughts. I acknowledged the fact that my feelings of being hurt, victimized, powerless, angry, and devalued were being created by me. I was self-sabotaging. My negative self-talk was my greatest problem, and if I could stop the self-talk, then that would stop my negative feelings, and I would finally be able to achieve the forgiveness which I so desperately needed for peace of mind and rest for my tormented soul.

At that point, I purposed in my mind to no longer focus on negative comments made to or about me. That was not an easy task considering the comments never ceased. I began to realize that words are powerless until we give them permission and power to either hurt or comfort us.

I decided to take control of my run-away thoughts by practicing a stop-thought technique. Whenever a negative thought entered my mind, I consciously stopped the thought and replaced it with a positive one. My strategy was to locate a list of what I referred to as power scriptures and created myself a scriptural toolkit. I used Scriptures for this purpose because I whole-heartedly believed that my answer would be found in the Bible, and that proved to be invaluable for my process. The toolkit consisted of a list of Scriptures addressing negative thoughts that plagued my mind in terms of interactions with some difficult individuals that had kept me stuck in my state of unforgiveness.

Sample Toolkit

When feeling victimized, read:

Romans 8:36-37 NKJV "For your sake we are killed all day long' We are accounted as sheep for the slaughter." Yet in all these things we are more than conquerors through Him who loved us. *(This helped me to remember that through Him I am always a winner, and that some things are not just about my feelings.)*

1 Corinthians 15:58 NKJV "Therefore my beloved brethren, be steadfast, immovable, always abounding in the work of the Lord, knowing that your labor is not in vain in the Lord." *(This reminded me that change does not always come quickly.)*

Hebrews 12:7 NKJV "If you endure chastening, God deals with you as with sons; for what son is there, whom a father does not chasten?" *(This encouraged me to look for insight revealed from my situation.)*

2 Corinthians1:3-4 NKJV "Blessed be the God and father of our Lord Jesus Christ, the father of mercies and the God of all comfort, who comforts us in all our tribulation, that we may be able to comfort those who are in any trouble, with the comfort with which we ourselves are comforted by God." *(This reminded me that I was not forsaken, and God would bring me comfort from my pain.)*

Psalm 71:20-21 NKJV "You, who have shown me great and severe troubles, shall revive me again, and bring me up again from the depths of the earth. You shall increase my greatness and comfort me on every side." *(This reminded me that greater days were ahead.)*

When feeling angry, read:

Proverbs 19:11 NKJV "The discretion of a man makes him slow to anger, and his glory is to overlook a transgression." *(This reminded me that it's my decision to be angry, and the ability to overlook an offense reveals inner strength.)*

James 1:19-20 NKJV "So then, my beloved brethren, let every man be swift to hear, slow to speak, slow to wrath; for the wrath of man does not produce the righteousness of God." *(This reminded me that my anger was not consistent with righteous living.)*

Ephesians 4:26-27 NKJV "Be angry, and do not sin: do not let the sun go down on your wrath, nor give place to the devil." *(This reminded me to evaluate my anger, making sure it was not mis-directed.)*

Ephesians 4:31-32 NKJV "Let all bitterness, wrath, anger, clamor, and evil speaking be put away from you, with all malice. And be kind to one another, tenderhearted, forgiving one another, even as God in Christ forgave you." *(This reminded me that to be forgiven, I must first be able to forgive.)*

Proverbs 29:22 NKJV "An angry man stirs up strife, and a furious man abounds in transgression." *(This reminded me that my anger had the potential to create more disagreements.)*

Ecclesiastes 7:9 NKJV "Do not hasten in your spirit to be angry, for anger rests in the bosom of fools." *(This reminded me that my quick temper was unwise.)*

Proverbs 15:18 NKJV "A wrathful man stirs up strife, but he who is slow to anger allays contention." *(This reminded me that I could control some disputes by controlling my anger.)*

When feeling devalued, read:

Galatians 6:3 NKJV "For if anyone thinks himself to be something, when he is nothing, he deceives himself." *(This reminded me not to feel entitled.)*

Romans 12:3 NKJV "For I say, through the grace given to me, to everyone who is among you, not to think of himself more highly than he ought to think, but to think soberly, as God has dealt to each one a measure of faith." *(This reminded me of the value of humility.)*

Romans 13:1 NKJV "Let every soul be subject to the governing authorities. For there is no authority except from God, and the authorities that exist are appointed by God." *(This reminded me that God was ultimately in charge of everything and everyone.)*

Matthews 10:29-31 NKJV "Are not two sparrows sold for a copper coin? And not one of them falls to the ground apart from your Father's will. Do not fear therefore; you are of more value than many sparrows." *(This reminded me of how valuable I am to God, and that nothing I had gone through had escaped His eyes.)*

Colossians 3:23 NKJV "And whatsoever you do, do it heartily, as to the Lord and not to men." *(This reminded me to keep my focus on pleasing God.)*

When feeling powerless, read:

Isaiah 41:13 NKJV "For I, the Lord your God, will hold your right hand, Saying to you, Fear not, I will help you." *(This reminded me that a powerful God is holding my hand and helping me to endure.)*

Isaiah 41:10 NKJV "Fear not, for I am with you; Be not dismayed, for I am your God. I will strengthen you, Yes, I will help you, I will uphold you with My righteous right hand." *(This was a reminder that the God of all power was my helper.)*

Isaiah 12:2 NKJV "Behold, God is my salvation, I will trust and not be afraid; for YAH, the Lord is my strength and song; He also has become my salvation." *(This was a reminder to trust God instead of my own emotions.)*

Psalm 28:7 NKJV "The Lord is my strength and my shield; My heart trusted in Him and I am helped; Therefore, my heart greatly rejoices, and with my song I will praise Him." *(This reminded me of the power in having a positive attitude.)*

2 Corinthians 12:10 NKJV "Therefore, I take pleasure in infirmities, and reproaches, and needs, and persecutions, and distresses, for Christ's sake. For when I am weak, then I am strong." *(This reminded me that even though I felt powerless, that did not make my feelings a reality.)*

Psalm 27:1 NKJV "The Lord is my light and my salvation; Whom Shall I fear? The Lord is the strength of my life; Of whom shall I be afraid?" *(This reminded me that only God has power over me.)*

I familiarized myself thoroughly with the Scriptures in my toolkit and considered them as power scriptures because they had the power to replace my negative thinking. Each time a thought entered my mind that I did not want to think about, I would choose an appropriate Scripture to recite. Reciting the Scripture took my mind away from the unwanted thoughts that were fueling my negative emotions.

Subsequently, practicing the thought-stopping process over time, I noticed something marvelous began to happen. The negative thinking began to occur less frequently, and the duration was notably lessened. Eventually, my thought-stopping process became almost automatic.

Once I made the commitment to work on myself and stopped focusing on changing the behaviors of other people, those negative emotions that I had battled with which had caused me so much inner conflict and confusion seemed to have dissipated as if something magical had occurred. It's a good thing to be introspective. I believe that it is possible to delay our own progress by focusing too much outward and not enough inward. I learned that it was more important to my well-being to take my eyes off that which I could not control and focus totally on what was in my control—that being my own emotions and behaviors. Thoughts, feelings, and behaviors are choices of the individual possessing them. I don't have now, nor have I ever had, any responsibility for the choices of other people. That was an extremely liberating lesson for me to learn.

I had come a long way in terms of climbing my ladder. There remained some broken rungs, and I had not yet reached the top. I was still climbing, yet in my process, and the Lord continued to bless me during my climb.

It's wonderful how He meets us where we are and walks with us until we arrive at the destination where we need to be for His purpose to be fulfilled in our lives. I think He was still teaching me that anxiety was not His will for me, and I could be totally free through faith, prayer, and thanksgiving.

He used me in that healing ministry to facilitate emotional stability for those who participated, including myself. Now that I think about it, perhaps that was His purpose from the beginning. Maybe the healing ministry was to assist me in crossing those final Broken Rungs on my ladder. The ministry was an avenue by which we developed richer and more meaningful relationships with God, each other, our spouses, and other relationships that were in disrepair. Getting healing from brokenness will open the door to actualize our fullest potential as we endeavor to live our best lives.

I believe that God inspired me to extend my reach in terms of facilitating healing of hurting people. I was already working as a professional school counselor serving the needs of students and parents. In addition to that, I secured a position as a Christian psychotherapist and worked part time as an independent contractor along with several other Christian therapists. After several years, I was motivated to enroll in a doctoral degree program because I thought that would give me a broader knowledge of the field of counseling and greater credibility with my clients at both the school district and counseling center where I was employed. Here again, I felt like God was proving himself to me and to those who knew from whence I had come. That little girl born to teen parents, who had lived a life of poverty and abuse, the one who could have been just another unfortunate statistic was still being elevated, defying all odds that had been previously against her.

I graduated from the university with a Doctor of Philosophy in Education Counseling and with the distinction of cum laude.

After receiving my Ph. D., I extended my reach in helping hurting individuals even further by opening my own counseling practice. The Lord blessed my practice, and I was never in need of clients. As a matter of fact, I had so many referrals, I often had to refer them to other counselors because I didn't have room in my schedule to service them all.

I believe that the Lord has placed some wonderful gifts inside each of us to be used for the perfecting of his people. We simply need to be willing and do the required work necessary for tapping into that potential which can often be hidden by scars from past experiences. Once I found the inner strength and courage to take an honest look at myself, and I identified what was holding me back and removed the distractions, I was on my way to my dream destination in life—helping others.

I had constantly felt as a child and young adult that there was more to life than what I was experiencing. I think that within my heart I always knew there was a greater call and purpose for my life. I had been hesitant to push forward in terms of actualizing that reality due to uncertainty. My feelings of uncertainty were rooted in fear, anxiety, and low self-esteem. Those are just some of the feelings that very often indicate that an individual is experiencing some residuals of past emotional trauma. I had been emotionally damaged and was at war with myself constantly. That inner struggle tormented me over and over again until I finally figured out what my problem was. Once I was able to identify my problem, and with the help of God, I mustered up enough courage, faced it honestly, and began my mission to correct it.

I retired from the school system several months after opening my Christian counseling practice. That provided me the opportunity to channel my focus in one direction, mainly healing the hurt and assisting individuals and families in getting their lives back on track. I was working hard, but it was extremely rewarding work. I ran my business single-handedly, scheduled appointments, counseled clients, did my own record-keeping, and billed insurance companies for payment. When we are serving in the area of our giftedness, even though the work may be intense, it is very rewarding, and I believe God strengthens us to perform the task.

I was finally walking in my purpose and it felt good. I cannot express the feeling of fulfillment that I derived from seeing a client walk into my office in despair and leave with hope to face another day. I prayed with my clients before and after each session for direction in terms of the most appropriate treatment plan.

It was my desire that each step I took would be directed by the Lord. I believed that this was His work, and I was not about to claim for myself any credit in terms of what He was doing. I saw myself as only an instrument that He was using to provide hope and healing for the clients who He directed through my doors.

Clients came seeking help with various issues ranging from blended family, marital and sexual abuse problems, and even children adjusting to issues resulting from divorced parents and being bullied in school. I believe that it was by the direction of the Lord I was able to develop a treatment technique integrating Bible principles and psychology which proved to be extremely successful in helping my clients gain the needed insight to make necessary changes for resolving their issues. I was convinced that, since I had experienced many of the issues that my clients were presenting with, I was able to relate to them with the level of empathy that they sensed was genuine, and I was able to develop trust almost immediately. Trust for someone who has been abused is usually a difficult undertaking. It was clear to me why I had endured my trauma experiences. Every one of them had been preparation for the work I was now performing for Him.

I was finally in a good place in life, doing what made me happy and seeing positive results of my efforts, then seemingly out of the blue, Norris came to me one day and shared that he believed he was being led of the Lord to relocate to Mississippi to do ministry. He was already working in ministry at the church where we attended, but said he believed strongly that the Lord was leading him to return to Mississippi. This was not news I immediately embraced. I was finally happy and felt like I was living my best life and at last flowing in my own anointing, doing what I thoroughly believed was His will. The idea of giving that up and moving back to Mississippi after being away for nearly forty years was not easy for me to accept.

Furthermore, my childhood dream had been to get away from Mississippi. Such a transition would change the life I had worked so hard to build. On the other hand, I did not want to be the reason why Norris would be in defiance of what he seemed to be so sure was God's will for his life. I was conflicted yet again.

My struggle to climb had taken so many years, and I had achieved a point in my process where I was happy, content, fulfilled, and doing a work that was important not only to me, but to the many people I was servicing. Why would God want to take me away from the work I believed so strongly He called me to do? Was God truly leading Norris to do ministry in another state, and Mississippi of all places? Surely my husband was making a mistake, I was thinking that there was no way this could have been from the Lord.

My mind went to many places. I questioned Norris' decision, and I also questioned why a loving God whom I believed had been with me, guiding me through obstacle after obstacle in preparation for the work that I was presently doing, and doing it quite successfully, would end my work assignment that He had so carefully orchestrated this abruptly. Had I misunderstood the reason for my journey or was my husband making the greatest mistake of our lives? There were so many questions I needed to resolve.

I began to take Norris' desire to relocate personally and fought hard not to feel resentful toward him for wanting to relocate. I felt like I had made enough career sacrifices while he pursued his twenty-plus years in the military. I had put my career on hold to travel with him and raise the girls. Now the girls were adults, and I finally had my turn at a rewarding career/ministry, and now he was asking me to give all of that up and make yet another sacrifice for something he wanted to do. I began to wonder if and when would it ever be my time? Was my passion not important to him? Did he think that my sole purpose in life was to serve him and the family? There were many questions floating around in my mind.

It took several years before I sorted each of my questions out and found peace with our next life transition. Norris never pushed me in terms of making my decision but brought the conversation up for discussion periodically. I knew that this move was important to him, and I wanted to be a good Christian wife. After much prayer and pondering, I finally agreed that it may be okay for us to make one final life transition together. After all, it is God who controls my destiny, and not me.

I began an online search for the best places to live in Mississippi. Norris' family owned approximately eighty acres of land in a remote area, but I already knew that living there was out of the question. I continued my online research and located the top ten places to live in Mississippi. We checked out each place carefully on the computer because I had a list of must haves for our new home. I decided I must have easily accessible medical facilities, restaurants, shopping, a quiet neighborhood, and a progressive spirit filled church all within a 5 mile radius. In addition to that, I wanted a home with a city environment, but country atmosphere. Safety and quiet were on my list of must haves. If I had to move, I wanted every amenity that I would be leaving behind plus a few extras thrown in just to make it all worthwhile. I had become accustomed to that type of living on the military bases and in our Willingboro community. I also wanted to have the warm, friendly experience that I remembered from old movies where I could share a cup of coffee with my neighbor, and if either of us needed a cup of sugar, she would be comfortable coming to me for it and vice versa.

After carefully researching, we narrowed our search to two cities and decided to visit them for a personal experience. Columbus, Mississippi was number one on the list because we thought we wanted to be near the Air Force Base. After visiting Columbus and getting caught in the most frightening storm I could ever have imagined living through, that area was no longer of interest to me and became a definite no. I couldn't see myself going through another one of those terrible tornadoes; therefore, Columbus was immediately taken off the list. We decided to visit our number two choice which was Southaven, Mississippi. We were both rather impressed with the community. In some ways, it was much like the area we would be leaving. I could see myself living there. We made two trips to the area before making our decision. The area had everything on my must-have list including the warm, friendly neighbor who was anxious to share that cup of coffee with me.

On our second visit to Southaven, we met with a realtor who showed us several homes in different communities. When we settled on a community, she then connected us with a realtor in New Jersey and the process of selling our home there and building our new home in Mississippi began.

The building process was exciting because this was our first new build. The other homes we had purchased in the past were existing properties. We had a wonderful realtor who sent us photos capturing each stage of the process from groundbreaking to the completed building of our new home. She even sent us a photo of introduction to our sweet neighbor-to-be who became one of my dearest friends. She and I shared many cups of coffee together. Our realtor also gave us a referral to the church that was on my list of must-haves. Things were coming together for us and, to my surprise, I developed an excitement about moving to Mississippi.

I provided my clients with appropriate referrals to other counselors and closed my business in preparation for relocating to Mississippi. When the time came to move, it was much different from the other times when the military did our packing. We were now civilians and had to do the packing ourselves or pay the moving company an additional fee to do it for us. It was no easy task locating a moving company with great ratings that would not cost us a fortune. We ended up spending several thousand dollars to move the huge collection of items we had accumulated over the years. Norris was ambitious and thought we could do the packing ourselves. It was clear that we were in over our heads and needed help. We gave it our best shot before realizing that the task was too great, and we needed help to meet our deadline. We did not have enough time to separate items to be discarded which resulted in the movers packing many items that were thrown away at our new location. What a waste of money. The house in New Jersey sold much quicker than we thought it would, and the new owners were eager to move in.

The movers completed the packing and loaded the moving van. Saying goodbye to the place where we had made so many memories made me sad. It was difficult closing that chapter of my life to open a new one at retirement age. I was not ready for complete retirement and had no idea what that would even look like. Work was a part of my DNA. It was how Momma and Daddy had raised me.

We arranged to have the moving van arrive at the new home in Mississippi on the day of closing. Norris and I came the day before. We spent the night at the Comfort Suites. We had stayed there before and knew that it was a comfortable and convenient location. The next day, the day of our move-in, we excitedly found our way to Bartlett, Tennessee to close on our new home. We could hardly wait to take ownership of our beautifully spacious home. Once the stack of papers was signed, we made our way back to Southaven, Mississippi to meet the moving van and our wonderful new neighbor,

Mary Ann, who lived across the street. She acknowledged later that she had watched through her window as we moved in, anxiously waiting her opportunity to meet us in person.

My dear friend, Mary Ann

Mary Ann possessed a warm, loving, and effervescent personality. We hit it off immediately, and she and I became best friends. It had been a dream of mine to have a neighbor with whom I could share conversations over a friendly cup of coffee, and I believe God gave me Mary Ann. I had a great time exploring the neighborhood and surrounding areas with her as we shopped for items to complete the finishing touches of decorations in our homes. She had moved from California several months before we arrived.

At a meeting with Mary Ann

Our new home was approximately twice the square footage of the home we had left in New Jersey, resulting in a lot of space I needed to fill. Meeting Mary Ann made my transition to Southaven much easier than I expected. It was like we had known each other all our lives, and we had so much in common that it appeared unreal. We began calling each other *Sis*.

There were special benefits that came from living in Mississippi. It afforded me an opportunity to see Momma more often than I had been able to while living in New Jersey. She would take a train ride from Chicago to Memphis each year to celebrate her birthday in April and again in November to celebrate Thanksgiving with us. Those were special times that I will hold fondly in my memories for ever. It was like she had two homes. She had registered and received her identification badge for the exercise classes held at the senior community center and had begun referring to our church as her Mississippi church.

I looked forward with anticipation to the times that Momma and I shared each year. Her special time always included a get-together with her two sisters who lived a couple of hours away. They had not been fortunate enough to spend much time together in Chicago. It was rewarding to get to know them again since I had not spent much quality time at all with them as an adult. I got to know my aunts again, and we developed a strong bond. We kept in touch with each other even when Momma was not present.

When I remember those special times spent with my mother, aunts, cousins, and Mary Ann sitting around sharing food, conversation, and laughter, I smile because I can see how God was still orchestrating His plan for my life even in that questionable move from Willingboro, New Jersey to Southaven, Mississippi. The plan was not just for Norris and me, but for Momma and her sisters as well. Sometimes it is necessary to look past our personal desires and focus on the total scene. Selfishness places us outside of His will.

Momma, Ethel, and Ann

As a little girl, I always dreamed of being able to provide an atmosphere for my Momma to experience happiness. At last she appeared to truly be happy. She frequently said, "I knew the Lord was not going to let me leave here without enjoying some of my life." Watching that childlike smile on her face warmed my heart each time she saw her sisters, went with me on a shopping expedition to purchase an outfit for her, attended an exercise class, enjoyed her favorite meal either at home or at a restaurant of her choice, attended a church service and got a chance to shake hands and talk with the pastor. The smallest things seem to have brought the largest smiles to her face. She would always say, "People don't have to do anything for you. And when they do, you should let them know you appreciate it." I never forgot those words or the sincerity in her voice when she spoke them. I learned from my Momma not to take any kindness for granted.

Life was going well for me. I had settled into my new lifestyle and was growing accustomed to retirement. I joined several ministries at the church which kept me busy and fulfilled my desire to pay forward the blessing I felt I had received from God. Momma continued to travel to Mississippi twice a year for her scheduled visits. In addition, I made trips to Chicago. It was wonderful spending quality time with her as an adult. We always maintained our relationship long distance, but it was truly special to be able to sit with her, enjoy our favorite beverage—coffee, reminisce about old times, and enjoy each other's presence on a regular basis.

Momma, church ready

My Story

PART XIII

**Now learn the parable from the fig tree: When its
branch has already become tender and puts forth leaves,
you know that summer is near.
—Matthew 24:32**

The knowledge that nothing stays the same is what I learned
from the parable of the fig tree. Grasping the concept of
change helped provide strength to cope with several very
difficult adjustments I would soon have to make—what the number
'7' in the Scriptures refers to as completeness. I think that number
was significant for me in terms of a series of completions. My dear
friend, Mary Ann, after seven years of being my neighbor and best
friend, moved back to California. Her move was best for her, even
though her return to California left a horrible void for me. I saw it as
a great gain for her family. I was happy for my Sis and truly grateful
for the seven years that the Lord had given me the experience of a
perfect neighbor. Her move did not represent completeness in
terms of friendship, but the perfect neighbor experience was
complete.

It was also during year seven that Momma made her last
train ride to spend her eighty-fourth birthday with us. During that
last visit, I noticed that she was not quite her usual spirited self. She
did not appear to be as energetic as before, and I could hear a
difference

in her breathing. There was a notable change in her appetite as well. It was during this visit when she told me that would be her last train trip to Mississippi, and we would need to come to Chicago to visit her in the future. She never admitted to being ill, and no one knew she had a serious health condition. She insisted upon independence, went to her doctor's appointments alone, and shared only information that she wanted us to know.

The next year, Momma's eighty-fifth birthday was celebrated in Chicago at her favorite restaurant. She had been diagnosed with pneumonia and hospitalized the month prior. Momma was a strong woman and continued to persevere without complaints. She kept her condition a secret for some time even though she was extremely ill. She packed a bag and spent time with me at the hotel, as she normally did on my visits to the city. My visits had become a mini vacation for Momma. She had a great time at her birthday party celebrating with family and her church choir members.

Over the next ten months she was hospitalized approximately three times and taken to the ER several times where she would be treated but refused admittance even though it was strongly suggested by the attending physicians. Momma did not like going to the doctor, and she disliked hospitals even more. Her condition continued to deteriorate. When my sister, Debra, convinced her that hospitalization was necessary for her to live, she unenthusiastically consented to being admitted. It was at that time when we finally learned the severity of our mother's illness.

I remember the day when my sister called me from the hospital, and the doctor talked to me explaining Momma's diagnosis. The doctor told me that I needed to come to Chicago to see her, because it was her professional opinion that Momma would probably need life support following a scheduled procedure that required anesthesia. The doctor's concern was that Momma might not be strong enough to wake up after the procedure. I remember the fear and overwhelming sadness that resulted from that conversation. I think my grieving process began at that very moment. I immediately booked my flight and went to Chicago. When I arrived at the hospital, the procedure was completed, and the transport person was bringing Momma back to her room. Instead of bringing her into the room and putting her into the bed as I thought was normal procedure, he stopped in the hallway. Before he could maneuver the cot into the room, Momma got off and walked into her room and greeted me in her usual cheerful way.

I believe that gave me false hope, and I refused to acknowledge the fact that her illness was as severe as the doctor had said. I camped out in her hospital room, and we chatted as we normally did on my visits to Chicago which helped fuel my rejection that her condition was terminal. I did not accept her diagnosis because I was in total denial and, at that time, did not have the emotional strength to accept the fact that Momma was terminally ill. I couldn't bring myself to even think of the possibility that Momma was leaving us. I think my denial was functioning at that time as a protective mechanism defending my brain from emotional overload.

Debra did her best to take care of Momma. She had such a strong personality that it was not an easy task to take care of her. She refused many times to go to the doctor. Debra called the EMTs several times when she was in crisis only to have Momma refuse to go to the hospital.

Her condition eventually declined to the extent that she was hospitalized for her final time. Norris and the girls were planning our fiftieth wedding anniversary celebration during that time. Rae was at my home finishing up details for what they had planned to be the celebration of our lifetime. I left her at my home with her father and sister, purchased my ticket, and flew to Chicago to see Momma. This time was very different. She was extremely weak and needed help getting in and out of bed. It was painful seeing her in such a weakened state with oxygen tubes in her nose. The strong, independent woman I had known for so many years was now unable to breath normally on her own. My poor heart was breaking as I watched her lie there virtually helpless yet still trying to remain strong. Momma never wanted to show any signs of weakness. She attempted her cheerful manner but was unable to pull off the deception any longer. Her secret was now visible for us all to see. She was seriously ill.

I remember the day when Debra and I met with Momma's physician and were told that there was nothing else she could do for our mother. I remember asking, "How much time does she have?" The doctor replied that it could be today, tomorrow, next week, next month, or next year. Those words infuriated me. I felt that old familiar feeling that represented being in a helpless situation. The anger I thought was under control was suddenly back and with a vengeance. I remember feeling intense rage. It was as if a volcano had erupted inside of me and hot larva was slowly oozing, heating, and consuming every fiber of my being. My heart was pounding so hard I could literally hear throbbing in my ears pulsating in rhythm with each heartbeat. I had not felt pain and grief that intensely since my Grandpa died. The emotions that I was experiencing prevented me from understanding what the doctor was saying. I interpreted her words as callous.

As I look back calmly, three years later, I believe the doctor was attempting to communicate that only God knew how much time Momma had, and she was merely speculating. What she knew for certain was that she had done all that she could medically do for our mother. Sometime during that whole agonizing ordeal, I experienced a minor heart attack. That information was revealed in test results performed several months later when I presented in the emergency room complaining of chest pain. I had been so immersed in my emotions resulting from Momma's illness that my own health had not been a priority, and I had consequently ignored some extremely dangerous symptoms. Thank God for His grace and mercy that protected me. I am thankful that nothing has the power to abort His plan for our lives.

After that upsetting meeting with Momma's doctor, Debra and I were informed that we needed to find an alternative care facility for her because there was nothing further that could be done for her at that hospital, and she was going to be discharged. The social worker met with us and gave us some referrals for facilities that our mother could possibly be moved into while she awaited her transition. We interviewed several and settled on one. When Momma was transferred to the facility, I camped out in her room for several days until we decided that she would come home with me to Mississippi. I don't know about Debra, but I was still in denial in terms of Momma's condition. I was holding onto hope that she still had a chance of survival. Momma and I talked about my fiftieth wedding anniversary and vow renewal that would be happening on the twenty-ninth of December. We also talked about her coming home with me and being a part of the celebration. At first, she was reluctant because she thought caring for her would be too much work for me considering my health issues. When I explained to her that I would have help to care for her she said, "Let's do it!"

I discussed the possibility of her travelling to Mississippi with the doctor at the hospice facility. He said if that was her last wish, I should do it. Momma had already said she wanted to come home with me, and if that was what Momma wanted, that was what she was getting. Debra helped me to research medical flights. We found one that had everything needed for Momma to make the trip. I made the arrangements. Momma and I flew to Memphis on a medical Learjet. It was like having her private hospital room in the air. A nurse and assistant watched over her, monitoring vital signs and oxygen as she made one final trip to Memphis.

When we arrived, the ambulance was waiting for us at the airport. Her room had been prepared with the medical equipment she required, and Norris was waiting for her at home. Norris loved Momma, and she loved him too. She always referred to him as her son and never as a son-in-law. He had worked with hospice making sure that everything Momma needed was in place when we arrived.

Momma loved Christmas. It had been a special time of the year for both of us from as long as I could remember. Norris had decorated the yard, and she got to see it and one of the trees that had been decorated in her honor. I had decorated three of them before leaving for Chicago.

She had been in transition for several days and was weak but alert when we arrived home. She knew she was in Mississippi. We came home on Sunday evening. Momma remained with us until Wednesday evening before she completed her transition. In my mind and heart, things were not supposed to have happened that way. I held onto unrealistic expectations. In my heart, she was supposed to get better. She was supposed to be at our anniversary celebration. We were going to renew our wedding vows and, since Momma had not had an opportunity to attend our marriage ceremony fifty years earlier, it was the plan that she was going to attend our anniversary celebration because it was going to be the wedding we never had. The children were planning the wedding of my dreams.

Momma and I had talked about that weeks before she was admitted for that final hospital stay. I had anticipated her not having the strength to walk into the event hall and had already acquired a wheelchair to transport her at the wedding. I planned what I thought to be every detail for us to enjoy the celebration of our lifetime. I loved making Momma happy, and she seemed happiest when her children were happy. I did not want to believe that she was gone before having enjoyed one last blissful event.

I remember while waiting for the ambulance to arrive for her body, standing by her bedside and just watching her, hoping that by some miracle the hospice nurse had made a mistake and Momma was still breathing. I moved her fingers several times at different intervals while I waited in the room with her. I stroked her face and even held a mirror to her nose hoping I would see mist on it from her shallow breathing. I was desperately seeking any indication of life. I needed to know for certain without any shadow of doubt that she was gone because I didn't want to give up on Momma until I was certain there was no hope left to hold onto. I knew in my head that she was gone, but I felt like I was in limbo waiting for my heart to connect with what I knew was true in my head. Momma was indeed gone, and I needed to find the strength to let go.

When the ambulance arrived, I was given additional time alone with her before she was put into a body bag then onto a stretcher and taken away. I followed the stretcher to the ambulance and watched as the driver placed Momma's lifeless body into the back of the vehicle. I stood in the driveway weeping uncontrollably as the driver slowly drove away with her. I watched until the vehicle was completely out of my sight. I remember that the nurse came outside to get me and said, "You need to come inside now. We can't have anything happening to you." I knew she was standing right next to me because I could feel her arm around my shoulder, but her voice sounded as if she were in a far distance. I felt momentarily disconnected from everything that was going on around me. My mind was racing, making it difficult for me to think clearly. I remember feeling extremely angry at the nurse and thinking she had done something to expedite Momma's transition. I was experiencing symptoms of emotional shock, but my level of reality was not compromised as it had been when Daddy made his transition. I did not expect her to get up and come back to us.

I was in a different place both spiritually and emotionally when Momma transitioned than I was when Daddy made his. I understood that whatever I prayed for must be according to the Father's will and not just mine if I were to get an answer. I accepted the fact that it was time to let go of my dear Momma. The pain of losing her was devastating. The ability to accept my loss and understanding the process did not lessen the overwhelming pain that I was feeling.

Family and friends attempted to comfort me with platitudes such as, God knows best, God doesn't make mistakes, and she's in a better place. I realized their words were coming from their desire to be helpful and this was their attempt to ease my pain; however, the words were neither helpful, insightful, nor did they ease any of my pain. Sometimes, it is better to simply say nothing. Being quietly present is often the best way to let a grieving individual know that you care. Clichés offered at a time when one is grieving can often come across as a lack of empathy. The worst thing that can happen to a grieving individual is for a friend to appear uncaring. My grief process was long and intense. I am convinced that it began the minute I learned Momma was terminally ill.

I didn't experience all stages of grief but seemed stuck somewhere between depression and anger for quite a long time. My feelings oscillated like a pendulum, back and forth, from a state of depressed emotions to a place of intense rage. That back and forth range of emotions continued several months before I finally settled at a place of acceptance. I think my acceptance came when Rae and I had a conversation, and she reminded me that there was nothing I could have done to keep Momma here because the power over life and death rests with the Father. Those words were not new to me but hearing them that morning ministered to a place in my heart that had been longing for comfort. I thank God for giving my baby girl those words for her mother that morning.

Grief is very real and must be confronted genuinely. God desires to bind up our wounded hearts, but we must approach him openly and sincerely present our brokenness to him in prayer. I did a lot of praying to God for strength to bear my pain and for understanding in terms of why things happened in my life as they did and when they did. I believe that God is intentional, and everything happens according to His purposed will. Therefore, I began searching for His purpose.

Our fiftieth anniversary party was scheduled to happen in thirteen days. My daughter, Rae, was chairperson of the planning committee, and she and her husband had invested a significant amount of money into the planning process. She came to me and asked if I wanted to cancel the party, considering the grief that I was experiencing. I hesitated for a while before giving her my answer and then remembered Momma's words. She would always tell me, "Enjoy your life." My heart was breaking, and my thoughts were running rampant as I struggled to make the decision in terms of whether I would choose to honor my grief and cancel the celebration, or if I would honor Momma's words and at least make the best effort possible to enjoy my life. I went back and forth in my mind trying to make the decision because there were times when I was unable to think clearly due to the stress resulting from my grief. I finally settled on the decision that I was going to, without hesitation, honor Momma's words, and we had our celebration, but not before honoring my Momma. I arranged a memorial service at her Mississippi church, and her Mississippi pastor delivered a beautiful encouraging eulogy. She would've been so proud.

Family members in the area who were unable to travel for the funeral at her Chicago church had an opportunity to show their last respects by attending the Memorial Service for Momma at her Mississippi church. After the service, we traveled with our children, grandchildren, and two of our daughters from another mother (my DFAM's), to Chicago for the final Homegoing and burial service. Momma was laid to rest in the style to which she had become accustomed. She was very stylish and loved to dress up in fancy clothes. Debra and I made sure she was dressed up and looked *presentable*, which was the term she always used when she got dressed up. She even wore a hat and fancy shoes to her final service at her Chicago church. It was two days before Christmas.

On Christmas Eve we made the trip from Chicago back home to Mississippi. Christmas Day was a solemn time. There was an eerie silence throughout the house. Not a single gift was under either of the trees, no Christmas carols playing, and no delicious Christmas dinner was served. It was as if everyone's emotional equilibrium was completely off track. Momma was loved very much and was being sorrowfully grieved. She had left an undeniable void in each of our hearts.

Christmas Day came and went. In our effort to follow Momma's advice to enjoy our lives, they moved ahead with preparations for the anniversary party which was scheduled to take place in only four days. A lot of hard work went into the planning for our anniversary party. It was designed as the wedding of our dreams from fifty years ago. They had done a magnificent job of pulling it off. Every detail was beautifully finished. I felt as though I had stepped into a fairy tale from the time the limousine picked me up at my home to transport me to the event.

My youngest grandson, Alijah, met me at the limousine and escorted me into the building. Walking in and observing the beautifully decorated and well-coordinated wedding venue was breathtaking. The color scheme was one of my favorite combinations—royal blue, silver, and cream. Our First Lady contributed to our evening and decorated the banquet hall in a fashion fit for a queen. She did a phenomenal job. Everything from the gorgeous flowers to the beautifully displayed wedding cake was superb.

Enjoying the reception

Lady Orr, Me, Norris, Pastor Orr   Alijah escorting bride, limousine driver

Two of my DFAM's from New Jersey had come to celebrate with us, and one of them greeted me with singing as I marched down the aisle to be re-joined with my husband of fifty years. I thought of Momma, and how this would have been the perfect evening if she could have been there. After a few moments with my feelings of Momma's absence, I refocused my thoughts, on "enjoying my life," just as she had told me to do so many times before. She was there in my heart. I simply was unable to see her smile.

Our DFAMS (daughters from another mother)

Many of the invited guests did not attend; therefore, we had a lot of food left unserved. We decided to donate most of it as a blessing to the homeless shelter. I believe that God does all things well. Having food left from our event may have been His plan for those in need of food to have the opportunity to share our delicious meal.

I have learned that when things are good, be thankful and celebrate, and when things are bad, pray and wait, because nothing ever remains the same. Change will eventually come.

I had finally begun to adjust to my life changes. Things were going well again. I was not missing Momma quite as much and had started enjoying life again. I was spending time with her sisters, and it was not feeling quite as strange not having Momma in the mix.

Left to right standing, Ann, Momma, Me. Seated, Ethel

The three of them had somewhat lost touch with each other over the years. My move back to Mississippi had been useful in helping the sisters reconnect. My home was the catalyst for that process to occur. The thought of the happiness Momma and her sisters had shared in my home gave me a sense of gratification, and I began to see real value in returning to Mississippi.

Year seven put in place a very difficult sequence of completions. First in the succession was when my neighbor and friend, Mary Ann, moved away, then my Momma transitioned, leaving a tremendous void in my life, and both of her sisters transitioned within months of each other. Each of those losses represented chapters in my life that were now completed and for which I grieved profoundly.

One would think that would have been enough in terms of grief experiences for me but not just yet. It appeared just as I started to get my emotional steadiness, I would be knocked right back down again. Within two years and two months, my mother and her two sisters had made their transition and were no more a tangible part of my life. Their memories remain fresh in my mind and heart, and I am tremendously grateful for the wonderful times that we shared.

There is an adage—*what doesn't kill us will make us stronger.* There was one more painful completion on the horizon that I would struggle to overcome. Three months and five days after my aunt, whom I had come to love as if she were my second mother, transitioned, I was in the kitchen when the phone rang. It was my daughter Rae calling from Texas. When I answered the phone, I could tell from her voice that something was wrong. A mother can discern in her child's voice when something isn't right. I was not prepared at all for what she was about to say. When she said, "Mom, I need you to sit down," I knew that something was seriously wrong. I followed her instructions, sat down at the breakfast bar in the kitchen, and asked hesitantly, "What's going on?"

As she proceeded to tell me that there had been an accident, I immediately detected from her tone that whatever she was trying to tell me was very bad news. She continued her attempt to explain what had occurred she said, "The policeman is still here. I'm going to let you talk to him. Where is Dad?" I said, "He's right here." At that point, she passed the phone over to the police officer who explained to us, in painfully explicit details, his assessment of what had occurred. Rae's only daughter, our only granddaughter, had just been killed in a horrific automobile accident. It was difficult to process the police officer's words. It did not seem at all real that this could be happening.

We had just spent Christmas in Texas and the whole family was together under the same roof for the first time in almost ten years. I wanted us all together, and the children and grandchildren had made tremendous sacrifices to make that happen for me. It had been such a special time of loving on each other, cooking together, enjoying food, laughing, and having an awesome time as a family. We were looking forward to the next time when we would be together again. Sometimes, we forget just how fragile and terribly uncertain life can be. Neither of us had a clue that, when we said our goodbyes before leaving Texas returning to our individual homes, that would be the last time hearing our granddaughter's, sister's, niece's, cousin's voice because she would be gone from this world and our physical lives four months and eleven days later.

Dress made with playing cards.   Muffin, Designer & Blogger.

We lovingly referred to her as Muffin. She was a beautiful and talented twenty-three-year-old with what we thought was a long and exciting life ahead of her. Our Muffin was an aspiring fashion designer and blogger, getting ready to make her mark on the world, or so we all thought. I just could not wrap my mind around the thought that she was gone from us so unexpectedly.

Muffin's tragic death was an abysmal shock. I was forced to draw from every lesson I had ever heard or taught in terms of God's love and comfort toward those dealing with emotional pain. My faith was not weakened but my heart was truly breaking. I was confident, however, that there was purpose even in this painful situation and, somehow, someway, there was a lesson to be learned that was going to be beneficial to all of us. I drew from my favorite scripture, the one that had given me comfort during so many painful situations in the past—*Romans 8:28 paraphrased: We know that all things work together for good to those of us who love God and have been called according to His purpose.*

I quoted that Scripture aloud frequently. It had been my source of comfort for many years and continues to give me comfort during stressful times. I didn't understand why my granddaughter had to leave us when she did, nor did I understand why she left us in the catastrophic way that she did. I prayed sincerely and searched for the lesson I was to learn from yet another dreadful loss. It was necessary for my healing to personalize the loss of Muffin. I needed to understand the *why* in order to move past my pain and be the support to the family that I felt I would need to be.

My Granddaughter was the fourth significant loss I had to overcome in less than two and-a-half years. I had many question that needed answers. I needed to know what all the pain and loss was about. I wanted to know why I was experiencing so many agonizing losses. I needed to know if there was a personal lesson that I would glean from all of this. It was as if I were being tested on the lessons I had taught so often regarding the power of God to provide hope and healing to those struggling with emotional pain. I did not want to fail this test. I felt that too many years had gone into preparation to fail at this point in my process. It was crucial for me to find my answers.

As I rifled through the archives of my mind and heart, I verbally acknowledged to myself and God that I had questions that needed to be answered and gave myself permission to ask God why verbally. I have a habit of speaking aloud when I am seriously contemplating something. There is something about hearing dialogue that brings a different level of clarity for me.

I believe it is okay to question Him if the reasons for the questions are not to challenge His authority, and my questions were not to challenge Him. I simply sought clarity so that I could process my feelings in terms of what had taken place regarding my only granddaughter and regain my emotional symmetry. Since God already knows our thoughts and intentions, He already knew the reason for my asking why. I believe He answered my question by inspiring me to read two Scriptures: Psalm 139:16, and Job 14:5 paraphrased: *Our days are numbered and recorded before we are born.*

Reading those Scriptures were as if I were standing in a dark room and someone suddenly turned on the lights. Immediately clarity came, and I had my answer. I understood and accepted the answer to my question of why our beloved Muffin left us so soon. I believe that the Lord allowed me to understand how each one of us is allotted a specific number of days on earth to make a divinely inspired impact on someone's life. Some may be given many days, and others may be given a few. God Himself makes that decision. It may be that those who are more gifted require less time to make their impact on the world. Muffin was among those highly gifted ones. Perhaps she only required those 8,525 days she was on the earth to leave a lasting impression on the lives of everyone who was blessed to know her.

I think about her every day, but not with sadness or grief any longer. My thoughts of my beloved granddaughter always make me smile.

I remember her last hugs that almost left me gasping for breath, her infectious smile, the beautiful earrings she gifted me with as she stated, "Every girl needs studs in her life, Gany," the special vegan dish that she was determined to prepare showing off her culinary skills just for her Gany that last time when we were all together, Christmas, 2017.

Muffin and I

Muffin's last hug

My special vegan meal

Partial family photo row 1. left to right: Muffin, Alijah, Hope. row 2: Rae, Me, Xavier. row 3: Amari

CONCLUSION

Life remains a fascinating journey, providing opportunities for countless lessons to be learned and shared with those in search of a more fulfilling existence. I have not yet reached the pinnacle of my journey, and I believe there are yet more heights to be achieved and lessons to be learned along the way. I believe that we all have been distinctively and intricately fashioned to become life-long learners and, as a result of that belief, I refuse to allow the fact that I am now well-seasoned in terms of years to abort my climb in pursuit of perfecting the divine purpose that He has in place for my life.

My intent is to continually keep my ear open to hear the soft whisper of His Spirit and obey as He directs me to offer a word of encouragement to anyone who crosses my path and that has a need and the inclination to hear. I endeavor always to seek relevancy and never 'act my age.' I do not see a rocking chair in my future. My plan is to keep seeking to fulfill His purpose. I have been an ardent student of life and have acquired many scars from my numerous experiences over the years. Each of those wounds has recited a valuable lesson that has not only proven useful to me personally but in my ministry of healing the hurt as well. It has been a tremendous journey thus far. I look forward eagerly and prayerfully with great anticipation to the next chapters of my life lessons and am confident that whatever they bring, God will give me the grace to endure as I learn even more valued lessons.

Experience has taught me that I am not a fragile object that needs to be protected, as my loving husband elects to do from time to time. We are both fully aware that I am no longer at high risk of shattering as I once was. Life has taught me that I am strong and resilient with God's grace actively orchestrating it. I have learned, though, it has taken much hard work, to confidently assert my individuality, make my own decisions, and not feel the need to be part of a pack just to gain acceptance any longer. I have learned to follow the lead of the Holy Spirit as we dance to our own tune and not so much the opinions of others that are in my circles. In so doing, some have misinterpreted my motives and taken offense because of my revised choices. Change has been both rewarding and difficult, not only for me but also for many in my immediate circle who were privy to observing my change. I think my transformation may have been met with resistance by some because it resulted in others having to adjust and perhaps make some modifications that they may not have desired to make.

I continue to parallel my life with a ladder to be climbed, but as I move closer to the top, something wonderful and exciting is being revealed. I am discovering that the struggle to maneuver over broken rungs is no longer an issue. My spiritual and emotional muscles have been well conditioned by the many years of rigid exercise acquired by maneuvering the shattered rungs on my ladder, and I have developed the agility required for my success. The former threat of slipping or falling has been removed. It appears that every broken rung is now beneath me as I move higher and higher approaching the top. Does that mean I will no longer have problems? Absolutely not! Problematic situations will most assuredly continue to occur while living in this world, there is no way of escaping them. But life has taught me to cast my problems on the Lord in faith, and He will provide the wisdom to manage complicated situations while allowing my peace to remain intact. I have learned that my perceptions play a major role in how difficulties affect me. If I perceive tough challenges as a means of opening up new avenues for acquiring information, then they are not viewed as problems. If I view them as something that will hurt me or someone I love, my outcome emotionally will be entirely different.

My life lessons have taught me to look for the silver lining in every situation based upon how I understand the Scripture that says, "All things work together for good." I have adopted those words as a personal philosophy for my life. They have grounded me during many stressful events and encouraged me not to give up in the face of my adversities, because there is something good to be found in each of them. I am convinced that if I look carefully and prayerfully at any situation, I will find a life lesson that will work for my good, one that is sure to provide necessary hope, help, or healing to strengthen and authorize me to face each of my difficulties victoriously.

Those distressing experiences of broken rungs did not have power to negatively affect my destiny. Thank God, I did not become a statistic as some may have predicted. Life's painful experiences did not leave me broken and bitter, but instead I believe they have made me better in every way by sharpening my spiritual insight, enhancing my capacity to give and receive genuine love, and look for value in all circumstances. I am convinced without hesitation that my life of broken rungs has molded me into the unique vessel I was ordained to become even before conception. I personally feel that my climb has equipped me to be formidable, yet humble, as I function in the roles of His servant, a wife, mother, grandmother, and great-grandmother to the beautiful baby boy that God blessed our family with approximately four months after our Muffin left us.

Holding our great-grandson, Xyzon

The value of my pilgrimage over the many broken rungs has been comprehensively for His glory and my story!

Xyzon at age 6.

Mary G. Patton, Ph.D.

www.ingramcontent.com/pod-product-compliance
Lightning Source LLC
Chambersburg PA
CBHW051157120626
46547CB00012B/1097